I C O C E A N

Pt. Barrow

B E A U F O R T

S E A

Martin Pt.

Colville River

k River

Kobuk River

C I R C L E

C A N A D A

A L A S K A

Fort Yukon

Yukon River

Fairbanks

Copper River

Dawson

kleet

kwim River

Anchorage   Valdez

Cordova

Whitehorse

Seward

Skagway

Cook Inlet

Prince William Sound

Juneau

A L A S K A

G U L F

Wrangell

Ketchikan

ninsula

Kodiak Is.

A N

E

Great Be Lak

Raymond Lufkin

HERE IS ALASKA

HERE IS
ALASKA

BY

EVELYN STEFANSSON

With a Foreword by
Vilhjalmur Stefansson

With Photographs by
Frederick Machetanz
and others

CHARLES SCRIBNER'S SONS NEW YORK

5189

ACKNOWLEDGMENTS

Grateful acknowledgment is made for permission to use the following:

Photographs on Pages 12, 15, 24, 113, 131, 135, 137, from Pan American Airways

Photograph on Page 19 from Caterpillar Tractor Company

Photograph on Page 55 from Federal Works Agency—photo by Highton

Photographs on Pages 100, 105, 137, 141 from American Museum of Natural History, New York

Photograph on Pages 92-93 by Norman Bel Geddes, courtesy of *Life* Magazine

Photographs on Pages 99, 116, 120 by Macracken from Three Lions

Photographs on Pages 101, 117, 121, 145, 147, 149, 151 by Simeon Oliver

Photograph on Page 107 from Department of the Interior, Ottawa

Photograph on Page 111 from Lomen Bros., Nome

Photograph on Page 125 by Lister from Three Lions

Photograph on Page 127 by Boury from Three Lions

Photograph on Page 14 from Three Lions

All the other pictures in this book were taken by Frederick Machetanz, Jr., on a recent visit to Alaska.

TO AN extent this volume is a by-product of Alaska research which has been done since 1932 for Pan American Airways and since 1937 for the United States Army. Through rather unusual circumstances the book, originally planned by another author, came to be written by a member of our research staff.

An important part of all our northern study is correspondence with men who live in places like Siberia, Norway, Arctic Canada, Alaska. One of our most valuable Alaska correspondents has been Frederick Machetanz. We discovered him in 1938 when he was working on his charming book for youngsters, *Panuck,* which appeared in 1939. On the surface this is a mere story, but it is told with such realism of background, with such obvious concern for the truth and with such clarity that it is no credit to us we were able to discern through it a man who knew the country, who had looked sympathetically upon both land and people, and who had derived ideas from what he had seen and heard. Then there was added the truth and charm of his drawings, which still remain the best action pictures of Alaska that have ever been published.

Since 1938 we have received from Machetanz a stream of valuable replies to questions on many subjects, among them climate, the possibility of airplane landing fields, the resources of the country, the natives and the colonists of Alaska and what has been happening to and through them. The correspondence soon began to be supplemented by visits when Machetanz happened to be in New York, and continued through his work on the second book for young readers, *On Arctic Ice,* 1940, a volume that lived up to the promise of his first book.

Then came the gathering of the material for the third Machetanz volume, which was to differ from the others in two main particulars. It was going to be based on a journey made specially for the purpose and illustrated by photographs rather than drawings.

It is our good fortune who have enjoyed and profited by the work of

Machetanz, and his good fortune, too, that his uncle, Charles A. Traeger, fell victim to the gold fever of 1898 and left his home at Kenton, Ohio, for the Yukon and Alaska, to become first a prospector, then a trader, now the oldest as well as the foremost white resident of Unalakleet, a town of which this book gives a full length portrait.

From the family home at Kenton, young Machetanz began to make summer journeys to visit his uncle, on one occasion passing a winter. Like most of those who live there, and like many who spend just one year, Machetanz found the winter even more pleasant and interesting than the summer—and became a complete Alaskan.

There were other summer journeys, finally the one of the present book in which he covered the south coast, the west coast, and the north coast of Alaska as far as Point Barrow, visiting also a number of the islands, among them the Aleutians.

In common with most Alaskans, Machetanz foresaw the coming struggle with the Japanese and knew they were going to be formidable. Therefore he began several years ago to urge preparation and to volunteer his own services to that end.

Machetanz was just back from his 1941 Alaska journey and was starting to assemble his photographs and literary material when Pearl Harbor struck and when, like many others, he dropped all civilian activities for duty with the armed forces. It was then he came to us to see whether a member of our research staff, with some of whom he had been dealing, would not take on the job of writing the book he had planned, arranging his pictures, filling in what gaps there might be among them, and finally turning over a useable manuscript to his publishers. In principle there were several of us, including myself, who would have been glad to do it; I for one could not volunteer, for I was fully occupied supervising research in the military field on behalf of both Army and Navy.

In view of the name of the author who signs the book, I do not feel in a position to go beyond saying that it was Machetanz who chose his literary successor and that I think he chose well.

Machetanz joined the Navy. Where he is now will naturally be a military secret, but there is little reason to doubt that his service as an officer in the Navy is in one way or another connected with Alaska.

VILHJALMUR STEFANSSON

TABLE OF CONTENTS

LIST OF ILLUSTRATIONS

HERE IS ALASKA

First prize in the sewing contest at Unalakleet went to this Eskimo woman for
the American flag she made entirely of reindeer skin

U P NORTH where Bering Sea meets the Arctic Ocean and Siberia and Alaska seem to be reaching out to join hands, are two little islands. These are the rocky Diomedes. Standing on Little Diomede you can see across easily to another hemisphere, into another day of the week! For Little Diomede belongs to the United States and is in the Western Hemisphere while Big Diomede is a part of the Soviet Union in the Eastern Hemisphere. Less than three miles of water separate them but through this narrow strait runs the International Date Line, on the other side of which is a new day. When it is Monday in Alaska on Little Diomede, it is Tuesday in Siberia and on Big Diomede. Some Alaskans call Big Diomede and the country west of it the Land of Tomorrow.

The Eskimos who live on the islands are inter-related and, with little thought of International Date Lines and boundaries held sacred by different

1

countries, they visit back and forth by canoe in summer, afoot in winter when the strait freezes over. This friendly exchange of visits is limited to natives; white foreigners may not land on Big Diomede.

In 1725 Vitus Bering, a Dane who had been in the Russian Navy for many years, was sent by Peter the Great to determine whether or not the Asiatic and American continents were connected. On August 16, St. Diomede's day, he sighted the islands and named them after the saint. A heavy curtain of fog prevented Bering from seeing what he had come so far to discover, the coast of America, and he turned back soon afterward without accomplishing what he had been sent to find out. What a trick of fate was this! Had the weather been good he would have returned to St. Petersburg triumphant, instead his three years of intense labor were considered wasted and the expedition a failure.

It is a common belief that once upon a time there was a land bridge between Alaska and Siberia by which the animals of North America and Asia migrated back and forth. The Diomedes, now placed where the distance between the two continents is smallest, only fifty-six miles, were probably part of this bridge. Later, man came from Asia. These islands were doubtless then the way stations of his voyages, as they have been since Bering's time.

Some believe that twenty, thirty, or forty thousand years ago, when man first came from Asia, he was able to walk across Bering Strait on an ice bridge that was part of one of the ice ages. This is not impossible, but far more likely the first human discoverers of America had boats similar to the cowhide curraghs in which the medieval Irish visited Iceland and the seal-skin and walrus-skin umiaks in which the Bering Sea Eskimos were making long sea voyages, with sixty or seventy people in each boat, when the Russians first came and told us about it. It is anybody's guess whether the first of these voyages were from Kamchatka along the Aleutian chain or from East Cape in Siberia to Cape Prince of Wales by way of the Diomedes.

The Diomedes have no harbors, either of them, but that would not have mattered, for the skin boats of that time would have been as easy to pull up on a rocky shore, as are the skin boats which the islanders use today.

Both treeless islands rise from beachless shores, with almost perpendicular sides. The village on Little Diomede looks, at first glance, like a medieval town. It has streets paved with cobble stones, complete with gutters for the

2

This might be a mediaeval village street instead of the settlement on Little Diomede Island in Bering Strait. The streets and gutters are made of cobblestones and the houses of rocks, held together with clay

water to drain off. Unlike most Eskimo dwellings, which are of earth over a wooden frame, these houses are, in the main, built of rocks held together with clay. Bits of precious driftwood are also used when they can be found. The roofs are of walrus skins.

In 1936 about 137 people dwelt on Little Diomede, most of them Eskimos and the Bureau of Indian Affairs school had thirty-nine pupils.

On Little Diomede a picture of Abraham Lincoln adorns the schoolhouse wall, while across the strait on Big Diomede a picture of Karl Marx occupies the same position in the Russian schoolhouse. Once a week movies

These Eskimos on American-owned Little Diomede are looking across to Soviet
Big Diomede Island, part of another hemisphere, where it is
a different day of the week

are shown on both islands, Hollywood productions on the little islands, and a
Lenfilm Picture, straight from Leningrad, on the bigger island. First the
islanders see one, then across the strait they go to view the other. One wonders
what they get from the mixture!

Big Diomede has one of the many scientific stations that the Soviets have
scattered throughout their Arctic territories, mainland and islands. The building of this one, in 1940, caused a newspaper scare; it was claimed that the
Soviets were creating a military base with an air field, with submarines, and
with thousands of troops. After several weeks of this sort of belief and talk,

4

*Landing a small boat with supplies on rocky Little Diomede Island. The supply
steamer may be seen several miles offshore and the island
on the left is Big Diomede*

Alaska's Governor, Ernest Greuning, flew so high over Little Diomede that
he could see all of Big Diomede. He reported that there were no ships, docks,
air fields, or other military installations, but that a single frame house was
being built. This was later confirmed by the U. S. Coast Guard, who pointed
out that since there were no harbors there could not be a naval base, and that
the island was too small and rocky for an air base.

As with typical Soviet Arctic stations, the one on Big Diomede pays most
attention to the gathering of weather information, so important to flyers,
and of ice information, no less valuable to ships. They also carry on studies

in various other sciences, like botany, zoology and magnetism. The weather information from the Soviet stations, sent out daily by radio, is of considerable value in forecasting the weather of Alaska and of the western parts of Canada and the United States.

On Little Diomede weather observations were being taken in 1940 by the schoolteacher.

The Eskimos on both islands live chiefly by sealing and walrusing and are among the best sea hunters and sailors that the Eskimos have produced anywhere. Compared to the rest of their people, they are good as carvers of walrus ivory and they excel in other primitive arts.

The Diomedes, however fascinating, are only a tiny part of the Alaska picture. Take a good look at your globe. Examine it carefully and set in your mind a mental picture of Alaska's position. See how close it is to Siberia and Japan; see how far north and how far south it extends. The Alaskan islands that lie between the continents of America and Asia are quickly becoming more and more important as civilization and wars move northward. Remember the Aleutians, the Pribilofs, Nunivak, St. Lawrence and the Diomede Islands. You will hear their names again. But first let us look at Alaska itself, and at the people who live there.

Little Diomede Eskimos paddling out to a ship in their umiak, or skin boat. Their village is built at the tip of the island and the white building just visible is the schoolhouse

ALASKA is a country of extremes — of the very old and the very new, of ancient Eskimo and Indian cultures and of modern gold mining and fisheries. Here you will find, side by side, glaciers and strawberries, dog teams and airplanes. A skin boat, the design of which has not changed for a thousand years, is fitted with the latest model outboard motor.

One fifth the size of the United States, its 586,000 square miles offer almost every conceivable type of climate and country. Between southeastern Alaska and the northernmost Arctic slope are magnificent snow-clad mountains, vast forests, broad prairies. Alaska has the third largest river in North America, the Yukon, coming in length and in drainage basin after the Mississippi and Mackenzie. It has many small lakes, no large ones.

Perhaps it would be well to stop off here for a moment and get rid of some of the common, untrue notions about Alaska.

7

One of the commonest of the mistakes is that Alaska is a frigid country, so chilled that there are no summers. But two thirds of Alaska is below the Arctic Circle, and at Point Barrow, the extreme northern tip of the Territory, the lowest winter temperature is slightly above the lowest records of North Dakota, Wyoming and Montana. In central Alaska the maximum heat of summer is about equal to that of New York City.

The persistent myth that it never gets warm in Alaska was exploded many years ago by explorers and travelers. But travelers have been known to tell "tall tales" and exaggerate the wonders of the places they have been, so we will use the statistics of the U. S. Weather Bureau, which are indisputable. The Bureau has recorded temperatures of 100° F. in the shade at Fort Yukon, 99° at Fairbanks, and similar highs for other places. Compare these with the highest recorded temperature of Palm Beach, Florida, which is about 96°.

Many travelers who have been both in the tropics and the Arctic say they have suffered more from the heat in the Arctic and from cold in the tropics. This is not as strange as it sounds. The heat in the Arctic is usually humid; in summer the days grow longer and longer until, for a short period, they are twenty-four hours long and the sun never sets. The heat is continuous; there is no cooling-off period. In the tropics, things have a chance to cool off during the long nights and do not start heating up again until the sun comes out next day. So that while the summer season is shorter in the Arctic than in the tropics, without the relief of cool nights it may seem harder to endure.

Usually when a tenderfoot goes to the tropics he expects it to be hot; so he is unprepared for the cold and usually improperly dressed for it. Similarly, people have heard how cold it is up north so the heat comes as an unexpected surprise. And the mosquitoes! Unless you have actually been north in the summertime it is difficult to visualize the terrific numbers of mosquitoes that exist and what a plague they are.

For some reason many people find it strange that there are mosquitoes in summer where it is very cold in winter; yet they know that mosquitoes can be very bad in the Adirondacks where winter chills go to 50° below zero, and in the Lake of the Woods country of Minnesota, where it is even colder. The truth is that 70° below zero at Fairbanks, Alaska, does not kill a mosquito any deader than 50° below zero does at Lake Placid, New York State.

There seem to be two main reasons why the mosquitoes are worse in the Yukon valley than in the Hudson valley.

8

Up around Albany the days which are warm enough to start germinating the mosquito eggs that have remained over from last summer are perhaps followed by nights so chilly that they kill the young mosquitoes; but at Fairbanks the sun in May and June disappears below the horizon for so short a time that the night does not have a chance to grow cold.

The second reason is as important as the first: Mosquitoes do not breed as well in a lake as in a swamp; they need many small puddles of water. In most of the Yukon valley the ground is permanently frozen when you get a little way down. Even when it is uncomfortably hot for many days running, the thaw may go down only a few inches. This means that the snow water from last winter, and the rain water of yesterday, cannot sink deep into the ground but stays near enough to the surface to make a swamp that may be bad from nearly every other point of view but is ideal for the mosquitoes.

Narratives of a summer trip in Alaska are seldom complete without the author's surprise at the suffocating heat and the numerous and terrible mosquitoes. Hunters, miners, in fact all who go into the country in summertime, have to wear mosquito netting over their faces to keep from being blinded by the mosquitoes and black flies. Gloves must be worn; sleeves at the wrist and trousers at the ankle must be tightly tied lest the pests crawl inside.

Mosquitoes impede farm operations somewhat during May, June and July, when field workers have to wear head nets and canvas gloves for protection. A number of farmers prepare smudge fires in the pasture so that the cattle, when tormented by mosquitoes, may stand in the smoke for relief. However the cultivation of fields, the drainage of pastures, lessen the mosquito scourge rapidly. You have no trouble, either, if you are in a town, or even a small village.

Many seem to reason about Alaska that because it contains glaciers it must be a frigid country. But glaciers can exist in any part of the world that has the proper combination of precipitation and a high altitude. Mount Kenia in Africa, right on the equator, has a glacier of considerable size on its summit; both Asia and South America have "eternal ice" topping their mountains in tropical and sub-tropical climates. Alaska's glaciers are chiefly on her southern coast and indicate not that the country is frigid but that the mountains are high and continually swept with moisture laden winds. There are no glaciers in northern Alaska because on the low, flat land there is little precipitation. The snow which falls there in winter is all thawed away during summer.

9

The northern two thirds of Alaska has, however, eternally frozen sub-soil. There may be a layer of a few inches to a foot of earth that thaws in summer each year, but if you dig down below this upper layer you come to the frozen soil, hard as concrete.

Alaska is, naturally, not alone in having frozen sub-soil. Half of Canada and an area the size of the United States in the Soviet Union have it too. Where the sub-soil is frozen you have no underground drainage and, as a result, you have thousands of small and large puddles and lakes. The larger of these make, incidentally, grand landing places for planes equipped with pontoons in summer and with skis or wheels in winter. Such lakes form, of course, only on rolling or level ground; where the country is mountainous the rain and thaw water naturally gravitate down the mountain slopes to the lowest levels. It is because Alaska is largely mountainous that it has proportionately fewer and smaller lakes than Canada and Siberia.

The cheapest means of traveling long distances in Alaska is by airplane. It is so cheap that even an Eskimo, who owns his own dog team and to whom time is of no value, cannot afford to travel by sledge between, say, Nome and Fairbanks. For lodging fees en route, and the cost of food for himself and his dogs, would amount to several times the price of an airplane ticket.

Alaskans probably fly more per capita than any other people in the world; their rivals in this respect will be found in the northern parts of Canada and the Soviet Union. With only one railroad of consequence and few roads, a traveler must often choose between dog team and plane.

Flying conditions in Alaska vary a good deal. The Panhandle, the south-easternmost part of Alaska, shaped as its name suggests, is perhaps the worst of all, but the south coast is often foggy and cloudy; so are the Aleutian Islands. Here flying conditions are generally unfavorable all the year round.

Along the Bering Sea coast of western Alaska flying is more favorable. Here the worst time is autumn; and thereafter, in improving ratio, are spring, summer and winter. On the north coast, facing the Arctic Ocean, conditions are much better in winter than in summer — in summer they are almost as bad as on the south coast.

It is in the interior of Alaska that flying conditions are especially good, averaging better for the whole year than the northern half of the United States. Autumn is poorest, then spring and summer. Winter is best of all.

In many parts of Alaska if you want to travel you must choose between dog team
and airplane. Strangely enough for long distances the airplane
is the cheaper method

Flying over Mendenhall Glacier is a never-to-be-forgotten experience

That this is the view in the Yukon basin was confirmed by a questionnaire sent to a number of veteran interior Alaskan pilots. Six out of ten of them said they would rather fly in January than in July; nearly all agreed that midwinter flying is safer than midsummer. More than half the pilots said that they would rather fly in Alaska than anywhere else they had ever flown. This was, of course, purely on the basis of natural conditions; for at that time interior Alska had few good air fields. These are now many, thanks chiefly to the Civil Aeronautics section of the Department of Commerce and to the War Department.

The chief reasons why the interior of Alaska is good for flying are climatic. There is comparatively little snowfall in central and northern Alaska. The skies are usually clear in winter and fogs are rare. The safety of northern flying depends partly on these air conditions and partly on the great number of lakes which are safe emergency landing fields for planes with wheels or skis. The air conditions are almost as good in summer, but the landing places are not numerous unless you have pontoon planes or flying boats. With wheels you would have to try to find a level sandbar along a river.

To Alaska's "bush" pilots, a circle of brush on the snow is the signal used by the vast, but sparsely settled, interior, which means that his services are needed. This is the "flag-stop" of the tiny settlements scattered along a pilot's routes, and a large part of his business is derived from going to and from such stops.

Many government agencies use airplanes in Alaska, among them the Post Office department for mail, the Weather Bureau for obtaining meteorological data, the Coast Guard for law enforcement and the protection of life and property. Perhaps the most useful service the airplane has performed in Alaska is in the role of ambulances for remote settlements, and in transporting doctors and nurses to the scenes of disasters and epidemics.

Many an Alaskan owes his life to the quick transportation to a hospital, offered by a plane, across a distance that would have taken weeks of traveling by dog team or any other means of transportation.

Airplanes are now commonplace even in remote villages. The teacher at Unalakleet, for example, no longer dismisses her pupils to watch the landing or take-off, and the children, hearing the roar of the motors, no longer shriek "Airplane!" and rush helter-skelter from the room. With the lowered cost of operation, and the improvement in flying equipment the plane has become an important factor in reducing the isolation of many an Alaskan village.

There are two railroads in all of Alaska; the Alaska Railroad, whose main line operates from Seward to Fairbanks, and the White Pass and Yukon, which runs through twenty miles of Alaskan territory on its way from Skagway to Whitehorse, in Yukon Territory, Canada.

The Alaska Railroad is government operated, and has four hundred and seventy miles of main stem. It operated with a deficit for a time but now shows a neat profit at the end of each year.

13

A steam-excavator on the Alaska Highway in Alberta, Canada

One of the stops on the Alaska Railroad is at Mount McKinley National Park where the chief attraction is the highest peak on the North American continent, Mount McKinley. This mighty mountain, which the Indians call *Denali,* meaning "home of the sun," is one of the most dramatic sights in Alaska. It is permanently snow covered for two thirds of the way down and reaches a height of 20,300 feet above the sea. No other mountain in the world rises so far above its own base.

Vast and beautiful McKinley Park is the farthest north and second largest National Park in the United States. It was created by an Act of Congress in February 1917 and covers 2645 square miles. From its ice-capped peaks and grinding glaciers to its foothills sweeping down into forests of spruce in the valleys, it is one of the most interesting and picturesque of our National Parks.

An aerial view of Mount McKinley, highest peak in North America

With Juneau, the present capital, and Sitka, the historic old Russian capital, it is probably the most visited spot in Alaska.

All of the glaciers of the Alaska Range rise on the ice-covered slopes of Mount McKinley and Mount Foraker. A glacier, incidentally, is not a stationary object but is a river of ice that is constantly in motion. If the flow of the ice is greater than the melting, the front is farther ahead this year than last and the glacier is "advancing." The glaciers in McKinley Park all appear melting at their lower ends faster than they move forward and are thus "retreating." The retreat is about one tenth of a mile each year.

The idea of a *new* travel route, the Alaska Highway, started back in the Twenties when a plan was developed for a motor road through the length of South and North America from the Strait of Magellan to Bering Sea.

Most of Alaska's shipping and business control is centered in Seattle and, to a lesser degree, in Portland, and San Francisco. So it was doubly natural that this tourist highway should be planned to run through the tourist-minded states of California, Oregon and Washington, extending in Canada through tourist-conscious British Columbia, which controls a large share of the business going through to Yukon Territory. The road was advocated mainly as a scenic highway that would draw tourists from all parts of the Americas.

In the Thirties, when the possibility of war became less remote, the promotion arguments began to backfire. The fact that the route was a scenic one meant that there would be grades, curves, trestles, bridges and tunnels. The claim that access to it would be easy through feeder roads from tidewater on the Pacific Ocean also meant that it would be easy for an enemy to destroy. A military need for a highway to Alaska would be largely in that we might not be in full control of the Pacific.

Emphasis had been on a *summer* tourist road and worry soon developed about the nearness of the Pacific, which would produce heavy snowfall, making the road difficult to maintain in winter.

Variants of the highways from Seattle were called Routes *A* and *B*. Now came the promotion of Route *C* which followed a recently established Canadian airline, the Yukon Southern from Edmonton via Whitehorse to Fairbanks. In 1940 United States taxpayer money began to be used for the development of the airfields at Nelson and Watson Lake. In 1941 the U. S. Army and other agencies of the U. S. Government with the consent of the Dominion Government, started the construction of a road to connect and service the airports.

The magnificent achievement of completing Highway C against what seemed like insuperable difficulties has been compared by many with the building of the Panama Canal; some experts even think it surpasses it. For much of the route from St. John to Fairbanks is through rolling country, some of it rugged and part of it mountainous. Another of nature's obstacles the Army had to contend with was muskeg, a slimy mass of decaying vegetable matter into which trucks and tractors alike sink and become helpless. One method of coping with it is to build what are called corduroy roads, rows of tree trunks laid across it, bridging the dangerous areas.

The virgin forests flanking a good part of the road provided abundant timber which was also used for building bridges and culverts. Paths were cut through the forests, continued over the mountains with Army Engineers working seven days a week, ten hours a day. The Army announced that by December, 1942 it will have completed its job of constructing a preliminary rough road and will then turn it over to civilian constructors for completion. By December, 1943 it is considered likely we shall have a finished all-year highway.

Because of the hilly nature of the country freighting on Route C will be, in the main, with rubber tired trucks, which will be expensive in rubber, petroleum and man power. No oil is produced locally on Route C; this will have to be supplied from the south, where it is already rationed, and from the Pacific, where we have tanker problems. These and other reasons have led to the consideration, not of any let up on the building or use of Highway C, but of the development of another route, one for heavy freighting.

This route, called Highway D, differs according to the season. In summer it goes by railway from Edmonton 200 miles north to McMurray where is the largest known petroleum reserve in the world, greater than all other known reserves combined. So this highway starts with an unlimited fuel supply which it can move down the Mackenzie River system, which points directly toward China.

In summer, freighting is by steam, tug and scow down the old established steamboat highway 800 miles northwest to the Norman Oil Fields abreast of Fairbanks, Alaska. Here North America's second greatest river, the Mackenzie, and her third greatest, the Yukon, are only 300 miles apart over a low divide. Crossing the divide brings us to the Yukon at Dawson, Yukon Territory, or a little farther downstream to Eagle, Alaska.

For five months, then, Route D has boat transportation, then comes the gap from the middle of October to late November when the rivers are beginning to freeze and during which time no traffic moves. With the freeze-up sledding begins and continues until April.

The winter route, by rail from Edmonton to Peace River, then goes north by sledge to Providence on the Mackenzie, northwest of which traffic is either on the ice of the frozen Mackenzie or on parallel roads through the forest. Where snow is available tractor-drawn sledges do a lot more freighting and do it cheaper both in men and materials, than an ordinary truck. A single tractor, for instance, can haul as much as 1000 tons of freight with a crew of four or five men where you need two men for every five or ten tons with trucks.

The Mackenzie valley road to the Yukon valley is historically the oldest. That was how the Hudson's Bay Company did its fur trade with the Yukon basin, taking supplies down the Mackenzie and carrying them over the divide and down the Yukon. Now it seems that endless chains of large freighting steamers will in summer take the place of the canoe fleets and of the small trading steamers, that tractor-drawn sledge trains will revive on this highway, and on a grand scale, the winter traffic of dog-drawn toboggans.

And this means, too, that there are two potential airplane routes from Edmonton to Fairbanks—by St. John via Whitehorse following Route *C*, and by Simpson, Norman and Dawson following Route *D*.

The principal interior highways of Alaska are her rivers. In summer they are liquid highways for the kayaks and umiaks of the Eskimos and the canoes of the forest Indians as well as for river steamboats; in winter, after the freeze-up, they are transformed into broad, smooth highways on which dog teams and tractors travel with equal ease. More and more freighting is now being done in winter by caterpillar tractors, or "cats" as they are called in Alaska, pulling long trains of heavily loaded sledges.

Alaska is the home of the third largest river in North America, the mighty Yukon. Only half known, and never fully surveyed, the delta contains numerous little known tributaries and countless islands and channels. At one moment it may be a "great, softly flowing mirror," at the next the shoal water of its mud flats is an angry, churning mass, from which all small boats must quickly seek shelter. This maze of islands and channels is on the southern side of Norton Sound.

At St. Michael, on Norton Sound, deep ocean steamers transfer their cargoes to the shallower Yukon River boats. In the days of the Klondike gold

Above—Over level country a tractor with a crew of four men can pull a thousand
tons of freight; a truck requires a crew of two men for
each five to ten tons of freight.

Below—In winter Alaska's main highways are her frozen rivers which provide
smooth trails for dog team and sled

rush, and for twenty years thereafter, this was an important transportation route, with large sternwheel steamers, drawing four feet, that ran upstream more than a thousand miles to Dawson in Canadian territory, where freight and passengers were transferred to boats of two-foot draft that continued three hundred miles farther to meet at Whitehorse the railroad from Skagway.

Thus there was, for passengers and freight, an endless chain of traffic which you might think of as moving in either direction from Seattle. You could go north along the Inside Passage to Skagway, up and over the divide by the White Pass and Yukon Railway to Whitehorse, down the Yukon by river steamer to St. Michael, and from St. Michael by a passenger liner to Unalaska and Seattle. Equally well you could reverse this direction, the only difference being that, naturally, the river steamers were slower plying upstream against a current varying from two to four or five miles an hour than when coming downstream with the current helping. For this very reason many experienced travelers preferred to make the round trip from Seattle by going first aboard the *Senator* or *Victoria* to Nome and St. Michael and then up the Yukon — it gave them more time to enjoy the romance of the great Yukon.

All this was upset by the government railroad from Seward and Anchorage to Fairbanks. The railway was in itself a fine thing, and the commercial making of its district, especially at Fairbanks; but it interfered with the Yukon River as a passenger and freight artery. The government road to Fairbanks took away just enough traffic from the Yukon River so that the steamboats lost money, and the service was curtailed until it practically disappeared. In 1920 it was the sentiment of the whole Yukon basin, with the exception of the immediate Fairbanks neighborhood, that the railroad to Fairbanks was the worst thing that had happened to interior Alaska, and the interior of Yukon Territory as well.

Along Alaska's intricate coastline, which is longer than that of continental United States, few towns and villages have harbors deep enough to receive ocean-going vessels. In many places supplies are delivered by having vessels anchor anywhere from several hundred yards to several miles from shore and lightering the cargoes on barges or small boats.

Alaska is like an enormous party telephone line, for almost every little village now has a short wave receiving and sending set. One of the most popular pastimes of an evening is to listen in on the short wave band of one's radio set to other people's conversations, exactly like the party lines in New England rural farm districts, where the means of knowing the local goings-on is to listen in on all telephone conversations on your line. This is done unashamedly and discussed openly both in New England with telephones and in Alaska with radios.

The short wave radio plays a new and important role in dispensing medical information to isolated villages where planes are not available and where weeks of old fashioned travel would be necessary for a doctor trying to reach a sick person, whereupon he might arrive too late. Emergency surgical operations have even been performed by schoolteachers with little or no knowledge of medicine, according to instructions, step by step, from a doctor a thousand miles away. Countless babies have been delivered by this method.

In peace-time, weather reports, so necessary to the aviator, are broadcast at regular intervals and by request. On the light side is homey gossip exchanged along with a new recipe for stewing reindeer meat. Chess games that sometimes take six months to complete are played, a move or two a day, by contestants hundreds of miles apart.

Why did the United States purchase Alaska? One history says that the chief reason was William Henry Seward, Secretary of State under Lincoln. Seward, whose far-sightedness is just beginning to be appreciated, reasoned that in order to properly defend the United States we needed Alaska to dominate the North Pacific, and Greenland and Iceland to dominate the North Atlantic. He advocated that we buy Greenland and Iceland from Denmark and Alaska from Russia; but he succeeded only partly in his plan. Negotiations were opened with Russia for the purchase of Alaska, a price of $7,200,000 agreed upon, and at 4 A.M., March 30, 1867, the Treaty of Purchase was signed by Secretary Seward and Baron de Stoeckl, acting for Russia.

Seward's plan to secure Greenland and Iceland were termed visionary and never accomplished. It was not until the United States began convoying supplies to Britain via the North Atlantic during World War II, and found how vital both those islands were for keeping the sea lanes clear of submarines, that Seward's genius was fully realized.

The town of Seward, named after the Secretary of State, has been a gateway to the interior as the southern terminus of the Government-operated Alaska Railroad. Big game hunters bound for Kenai Peninsula and Kodiak Island usually outfit here. Seward's port is open all year and even floating ice is a rare sight.

From the purchase until 1897 was a black period of lawlessness in Alaska's history. With no civil law or administration for maintaining order, murder, burglary and drunkenness were the order of the day. The gold stampeders in the late 1890's and 1900's, although without civil authority, created their own form of local self-government, on the order of New England town meetings. Together with such sporadic administration as was possible through the Coast Guard and through Army posts, this served until 1912, when the Alaskan legislature was created.

Fishing and canning, mining, fur trapping and breeding, transportation and farming; these are the ways Alaskans earn their living. Recently many have gone into domestic and personal services which cater to the normally large tourist trade.

When people think of Alaska they almost automatically think of gold: gold dust, gold rush, gold mining. But while gold mining is a great industry in Alaska, it is not as large or as important as the fisheries.

Millions of salmon are caught and canned each year and represent ninety per cent of the total fisheries output. Cod, herring and halibut are also caught in large numbers. Legislation has been passed limiting the methods of fishing, and fish hatcheries have been opened.

Whaling was once among the chief industries of Alaska, but is now represented by a tiny and unromantic remnant at Akutan Island; small whales are shot from big boats with cannon, instead of the harpooning of the great bowheads from rowboats. What they seek now is oil used for food; the rest of the carcass is ground up for fertilizer. It was far different in the old days.

The "gold period" of Alaska whaling was that of the bowhead or whalebone whale. At first, and especially before the Civil War, oil was taken as well as the bone, the oil used for lamps. A Yankee fleet engaged in this sort of whaling was pursued by Confederate privateers and destroyed on the north coast of Alaska between Point Barrow and Icy Cape. This last battle of that war took place several months after Lee surrendered, for those were not the days of the radio. It practically ended the search for the oil whale in these waters, partly because the New England owners were ruined but more because kerosene was coming in to take the place of whale oil for the lighting of homes.

Nine Eskimos on a dead whale's back

The revival of whaling after the Civil War depended on whalebone, the two chief markets of which were in corsets for women and in buggy whips for men, although there was a considerable use by tailors to make men look square shouldered and broad shouldered.

The whaling ships used to go up through Bering Straits and east in summer along the north coast of Alaska, returning the same autumn. In 1889 the first ships wintered, at Herschel Island just west of the delta of the Mackenzie River in what was then supposed to be U. S. territory. The *Thetis* a Revenue Cutter, as Coast Guard ships were then called, determined that the harbor was in Canadian territory, but still the industry which continued may fairly be called Alaskan, for many of the whales were caught north of Alaska and north of Bering Straits.

Above—*Shrimpboat fishing. Fishing is the important industry of Alaska.*
Below—*Salmon is prepared for drying by cutting out the backbone and ribs and removing the head. It will then be hung on a rack to be dried by the wind*

Above—*A young Eskimo hanging salmon on the fish rack to be dried by the wind*
Below—*An Eskimo family at Unalakleet catches about 4,000 salmon each sum-*
mer. Here they are being wind dried, with a canvas cover
protecting them from rain

The ships used to winter two or three times on a voyage. The number of men per ship was usually forty-nine, because the law required that a ship with fifty or more had to carry a doctor. The largest catch on record was sixty-nine whales on a voyage; the largest whale gave two thousand pounds of bone, netting ten thousand dollars at five dollars per pound. Fortunes grew rapidly. Everybody got rich except the men before the mast who worked on a percentage and usually managed to spend most of it on what the skipper sold them from the slop chest. Theirs were the small percentages, called lays. The captains had big lays and sometimes were able to buy their own ships eventually. The main proceeds went to the owners.

This romantic and lucrative business came to a sudden close in 1906. That year more than a dozen ships had wintered at Herschel Island, or points east; thereafter no more than two or three ships wintered, and these devoted themselves almost wholly to trading, which had been ignored during the whaling days except as a sideline, chiefly to secure fresh meat from the Eskimos or to pay them for services.

The failure of the whalebone industry was caused by three things which happened together: Women stopped wearing heavily-boned corsets because of a change in fashion, men stopped using buggy whips because the automobile was coming in, and somebody invented a substitute for whalebone that could stiffen acceptably the shoulders of men's coats. Whalebone dropped in price from four or five dollars the pound to fifteen or twenty cents, and, indeed, could not be sold at any price except in very small quantities.

Gold mining is the second industry of Alaska. In a single year, 1937, over $20,000,000 worth of that precious yellow metal was produced. Gone, though, are the days when a prospector can go out with his pan and cradle, as he did during the days of the gold rush, and come home in the evening with a poke large with dust and nuggets. Gold mining in Alaska today is a highly mechanized industry carried out on a large scale, usually by corporations with office and stockholders outside Alaska.

Besides gold, Alaska has large supplies of copper. There are silver, platinum, tin, marble, coal and oil.

From Alaska's earliest days, fur has played an important role. The first Russians that set foot on Alaska were seeking furs; today it is the third ranking industry. Many miners, fishermen and other seasonal workers trap fur

26

bearing animals during the winter. In the order of the importance the principal animals are fox, marten, mink, otter, wolverine, ermine, muskrat, beaver, lynx, land otter, polar bear, and black, brown and grizzly bears.

Fur farming, too, has become an important industry, especially the blue fox ranches on the Aleutian Islands and the smaller islands in Prince William Sound and southeastern Alaska. Silver fox and mink farming have also been successful, one reason being the abundance of fish which can be the main item in the diet of those animals.

Today the fur seal herds are completely under government control, and Coast Guard vessels follow and protect them during their migrations. Sea otters, which were almost extinct when the Government forbade the killing of them, are slowly gaining. The killing of walruses and sea lions is prohibited, unless by natives for food and clothing or by miners and explorers in need of food.

That narrow strip of southernmost Alaska, that adjoins the British Columbia coast like a narrow hallway leading to Alaska proper, is called the Panhandle. In its intricate maze of islands and passes lie three of Alaska's largest cities: Ketchikan, Juneau, the present capital, and Sitka, the old Russian capital. The "inland passage" from Seattle, famous for its beauty, threads its way through these islands.

The Eskimos

ALL THE "first families" of Alaska were originally either Eskimo or forest Indian. In the southeastern part of the country lived the Tlingit Indian tribes, possessed of a great unwritten literature and a complicated social life. Their houseposts, made usually of huge cedar trunks, were often elaborately carved and painted to represent the family totem, or family tree. Most of these totem poles have been carefully restored and may be seen today at Sitka National Monument Park and elsewhere.

Living today in southeastern Alaska are about three thousand Tlingits, about five hundred Tsimsheans, most of whom are at Metlakatla, and about six hundred Haidas. The Tsimsheans and the Haidas, whose fathers migrated from British Columbia to Alaska, are small segments of large tribes still residing in Canada. Little remains today of the old Indian cultures, for these sons of great warriors earn their living by working in the white man's modern canneries and factories. Many of their crafts have been forgotten, but the Bureau of Indian Affairs is trying to revive them.

In the interior of Alaska live about five thousand Tinneh or Athapascan Indians who are essentially fur trappers and caribou hunters. They resemble the southeastern Indians more than they do the Eskimos.

On Alaska Peninsula and until very recently (July, 1942) in the Aleutian Islands lived about four thousand Aleuts, first cousins of the Eskimos, with a similar language and culture. They are the survivors of a once great nation; but, with their largely Russian blood and their devotion to the Greek Orthodox Church, they often seem more Russian than Eskimo.

By far the largest group of natives in Alaska are the true Eskimos, but although they number well over fifteen thousand they are only a small remnant of what they were a hundred years ago.

The Eskimos are good-humored, honest and self reliant people who dwell along the Arctic Ocean and Bering Sea, as well as in the deltas of the rivers and, in some cases, well up the river valleys, especially along the Colville, Noatak and Kobuk. Their present economy is in some districts based largely on the reindeer introduced into the Territory for that purpose more than forty years ago by the Bureau of Education. They are generally hunters of the caribou, mountain sheep and moose; of the polar bear, seal, walrus and whale.

The Eskimos have always been to an extent fishermen, particularly on the Bering coast; through the influence of the Russian America Company, of the Hudson's Bay Company, and of the Free Traders, as competitors of the two great companies used to be called, they have become fur trappers as well.

North of the Arctic Circle most of the people live, for at least part of the year, on or near the coast. On the great inland prairie the population is now very sparse, but only fifty years ago this plain was inhabited by ten or perhaps even twenty times as many Eskimos as now.

Long ago, "before the coming of the white man" the people of the coasts of northern Alaska depended chiefly on seal and whale, those of the interior lived mainly on caribou supplemented by a few birds and fish from the inland lakes and rivers. In the mountains a comparatively few lived mainly on sheep.

The coastal Eskimos used the plentiful seal, walrus and whale oil for fuel and light; the inland Eskimos depended in the main on spruce, alder

29

and willow for fuel. In their camps they burned for light caribou tallow, or oil which they purchased from the coastal people, largely for skins of caribou and sheep. Once a year, usually in late winter, they would make a journey to hunt seals, to visit and to trade.

The western and southern coasts of Alaska were in fairly close touch with the Russians, and with other white men, in the eighteenth century, and the interior similarly in the early nineteenth. The north coast of Alaska had sporadic whalers a hundred years ago but did not have a resident trader until Charles D. Brower settled at Barrow in 1884. Generally, throughout Alaska, the missionaries followed close on the heels of the traders.

The whalers and traders needed fresh meat for food and to ward off the dreaded scurvy. They had never heard of vitamins, but the sea captains knew that if they had fresh meat (which does contain the necessary vitamins) they and their crews would keep in good health. So they offered lures of every sort to get the Eskimos to hunt for them.

Soon after the first contact between the two peoples, the natives of Alaska began to die in great numbers from various diseases brought in by the whites. This was no doubt so throughout Alaska, but we know the story best from the Eskimos. The deadliness of the new sickness was due to its newness — neither the ancestors of these prairie Indians nor those of their forest cousins had ever been afflicted with any of them, so there could be no inherited immunity.

It is a common belief that the deadliest scourge that has ever swept the native peoples of the New World was smallpox, and this may indeed be true; but so far as we really know the history of Alaska by far the deadliest plague has been measles. There was an epidemic around the turn of the century which killed not less than one quarter of the people in any village we know about and which, according to a report which we believe authentic, killed ninety-eight out of ninety-nine people of one village, the only survivor being a girl of about six. The second epidemic, which came a few years later, may have killed from ten to twenty per cent; the third killed only a few, and now the danger of measles to the comparatively small Eskimo remainder is not much greater than to us. This is because only those survived the first and second epidemics who had an immunity against measles, which they transmitted to their children as they would transmit other characteristics, such as form of nose or chin. At any rate, such is our current explanation.

30

This totem pole is the "family tree" of a southeastern Alaskan Indian

You occasionally hear it said in Alaska that a death from measles was really a death from pneumonia, and that the pneumonia was caused by the chill and damp climate. "The dumb natives," say these critics, "would not stay in the house and keep warm." That explanation seemed reasonable in Alaska; but measles has had a similar death rate in the tropical islands of the Pacific. This plague seems to be equally fatal wherever it goes, so long as the territory is equally new.

It is also a fairly common Alaska view that the measles death rate could have been greatly decreased if the natives had followed the directions of white men, who were in certain of the communities, or "if they had had good medical attendance." But Dean Vaughan of the University of Michigan Medical School, a foremost epidemiologist, has said that if, in the South Pacific or Alaska, medical science had had several years of warning that the disease was coming, but without chance for establishing a quarantine against it, then all the rest the doctors could have done — through hospitals, sanitation and medical treatment — would surely have lessened the death by no more than ten per cent. Other epidemiologists have said that the effect of any treatment known in 1900 would have produced only a negligible effect.

It is not clear what the relative deadliness among the other diseases has been. Influenza epidemics show death rates higher among the Eskimos than among us. The "flu" of 1919 was on the west coast of Alaska perhaps twice as dangerous to Eskimos as to whites, but it was nothing to compare with the measles records.

Most Eskimo deaths are now caused by tuberculosis, about which there is debate. Some think that the disease was always there but that it was kept in check, as long as the natives retained their own way of living, by wholesome food, by comparatively sanitary housing and by the generally favorable conditions of life. Others believe that tuberculosis did not exist among the Eskimos until introduced by whites in historic times, and that the greater death rate among them than among us is accounted for by the newness of the scourge, as with measles.

In one respect only have the whites brought with them a great improvement, insofar as mortality figures go. This has been through reducing the death rate at childbirth both for mothers and children.

Among most Eskimos it was not permissible that anyone be present when a child was being born. The most that could be permitted, in some districts, was that a woman's mother might be outside the house shouting advice in to her daughter. In other districts not even this was permissible. They did have one advantage, even in childbirth cases, that the bacteria which cause infections, including "blood poisoning," were rare or absent. In the Arctic and sub-Arctic practically every wound is a clean wound; there is little need there for things like iodine in your medicine kit, except in towns or where the people live in good part on imported things, where (we think) the bacteria that make wounds fester have come in with the packages.

The rapid decline of population in northern Alaska, although well understood by the few white men who really knew the country, was not apparent to the summer visitor. The inland was perhaps never as densely populated as the coast, but a hundred years ago there were a good many people on the Colville, the Noatak, the Kobuk, and on the prairie north of the Brooks Range. These, as we have indicated, visited the coast only in families and small groups, chiefly in late winter.

For some time the coastal people had a great deal more to do with the whites than did the inlanders, becoming more dependent on their foods and wares. With this association and dependence came the diseases that killed them off. For a time the inlanders acquired a taste for association with the white man, especially for trading with him, about as rapidly as the coastal people died off, so that when the census-takers came down along the shore from Point Hope through Icy Cape, Wainwright and Barrow, they found villages of the same size as ten years before, perhaps even growing. Because they were lazy, or because they did not know any better, these census-takers usually paid no attention to whether the heads they counted were those of native villagers or of people who had just moved in from the mountains and plains to trade with and work for whalers. They merely reported how many people they had counted on the coast.

Through this naiveté of the census-takers it is possible, if you are willing to shut your eyes to the rest of the evidence, to prove by government reports that the population of northern Alaska has been stationary for forty or fifty years. But if you can speak Eskimo, in which case you are one of less than a dozen whites in North America, or if you have a good interpreter, which is easy to manage, you can find out this year, by talking with people at villages like

Chief Shake of the Tlingit Indians

She remembers when Russia sold Alaska to the United States

Two jolly members of the younger set.

Barrow or Wainwright, that the fathers and mothers of more than half of them, their grandfathers and grandmothers, belong to one or another of the inland groups — they are Oturkagmiut, Nunatagmiut, Itkiligmiut, or something of the sort. Those who are descended solely, or even mainly, from coastal stock are but a small fraction of all the people you can now find, even though the coastal population was perhaps once heavier than that of the interior.

36

Perhaps we had better say explicitly what has been implied, that the Eskimos are not fading away towards disappearance. Some years ago, perhaps as many as ten or twenty years, was the lowest ebb. By then the various new diseases had each killed away those most susceptible to it, leaving as fathers and mothers of the next generation only those who were partly or completely immune, able to transmit their immunity to their descendants. About the only disease to which this does not seem to apply is tuberculosis. It seems now, especially if you are firm believer in the immunity doctrine, that it should not be many generations until the tuberculosis record of the Eskimos is no worse than ours. When that time comes they will begin to increase as rapidly as we do. Meantime they are increasing a little.

During the years when the Eskimos of Alaska were getting fewer and fewer, those of Greenland were increasing at a rate comparable to that of white populations elsewhere. This difference is partly due to the difference in the policies of the United States and of Denmark. The Danes enforced a quarantine to protect their Eskimos from outside influences and encouraged them to retain their old economy and culture. Until recently we Americans have taken neither this nor any other leaf from the book of Danish colonial administration.

A new plan now being put into effect by the Bureau of Indian Affairs is designed to give the native peoples of Alaska a better understanding and use of their native environment and to give them the knowledge and skills necessary to make profitable contacts with the better elements of the white man's civilization. It aims to preserve for the use of the Eskimos their native foods, clothing, industries and culture. In some cases this means teaching Eskimos methods of sewing, sled-making and hunting, which had been forgotten. They will be encouraged to take pride in doing things the Eskimo way and trained also to meet the inevitable white competition.

The Eskimos and the other Indians of Alaska were formerly wards of the Government; they had no rights of citizenship but the Government was pledged to look after their welfare. But in 1924 an Act of Congress provided that "all non-citizen Indians, born within the territorial limits of the United States, shall be citizens," and that the granting of citizenship shall not in any way affect the right of an Indian to tribal or other property. Some have contended that the Eskimos are not Indians and would not come under this law, but it has been ruled that the law does apply to them. It would be strange if the law did

37

not, for biologically and anthropologically they are of the same race, just as Swedes and Spaniards are both members of the white race.

Until their contact with Europeans, when births began to be recorded by missionaries and school teachers, the Eskimos did not know how old they were, except in a vague way, and considered it unimportant. They did not reckon age by years but by terms like our infant, child, youth, adult. This was a matter of social outlook, though it has been said by whites that the Eskimos had trouble with counting. That idea cannot have come from any close knowledge of the Alaska Eskimos; except for imbeciles, of whom they have a few just as we do, you will not meet anyone who cannot count at least to four hundred. They count by twenties, using both fingers and toes where we use only the fingers, so that what corresponds to our 100, ten times ten, is 400, twenty times twenty. Occasionally some Eskimo might tell you that it was not possible to count higher than 400, but if you pressed him he could usually devise an extension. It was no more logically necessary for them to stop at 400 than it is for us to stop at 100.

The Eskimos had nothing like our miles, but reckoned a journey in fractions of a day; if it was more than two days then they usually spoke in number of days. True, many whites in Alaska have had the impression that Eskimos reckoned journeys by sleeps, one sleep being two days, two sleeps three days, and so on. But this appears to be an idea which the whites brought with them, perhaps having derived it from youthful enjoyment of stories by James Fenimore Cooper. The Eskimos had no trouble in getting the Fenimore Cooper idea, and now there are many of them who, even among themselves, will reckon a journey in sleeps.

An idea, or at least a word, which they did not have was "year." They spoke of spring, summer, autumn and winter, and they reckoned years either in winters or in summers.

They had months in the sense of moons, and usually knew that there were thirteen in the complete cycle. But some of them would tell you that there were eight moons, nine moons, ten moons, according to what part of Alaska you were in, and then they would give the moonless period, which would be the summer, when the night was so bright that the moon could not be seen.

One of the strangest ideas to an Eskimo is that of our cardinal points. Their thinking in this respect is not governed by the sun; it is governed by the shoreline, for most of them are coastal people. So their directional words are up the coast, down the coast, inland and out to sea. This has been confusing to those whites who did not know the language thoroughly, and you find in the vocabularies of Eskimo words copied down by the average traveler such things as that *nigerk* is an east wind. But if you examine enough vocabularies you find one of them saying *nigerk* is an east wind, another that it is a west wind, a third that it is a south wind and a fourth that it is a north wind. Of course the meaning is that *nigerk* is a wind that blows up the coast. Similarly *kanangak*, which has many meanings in many published vocabularies, has only one meaning to the Eskimos. It is a wind from inland; which may be north, south, east or west, according to where you are.

As we have implied, the Eskimo language is perhaps the hardest of all languages in the world to learn, which is why you get so many strange, or at least different, interpretations from different travelers. The only whites who learn Eskimo are a few missionaries who have been studious and who have lived long in the country, a half dozen scientists and a few whites who have married Eskimo women. Only from these few can you get a discriminating understanding of how the Eskimos think and of what ideas are and are not within their scheme.

Eskimos as a rule are quick-witted and intelligent, showing a remarkable capacity for appreciating and learning useful things, especially mechanical arts.

One explorer tells of an Eskimo who possessed a dollar watch, which stopped after two years of use. Its owner proceeded to open the back of it and take it apart, piece by piece. After carefully cleaning each part he put it back together again so that it worked perfectly, although he had never taken a watch apart in his life. Equally remarkable tales are told of their ingenuity in repairing outboard motor engines they have never seen before, which has astounded people who have thought of them vaguely as a "primitive" people.

As you go north toward the Arctic Circle log cabins become fewer as the spruce forests disappear, and sod houses more frequent. When there are no longer enough trees to make even the frames of these earthen houses, driftwood is substituted. Whales' bones are sometimes used, perhaps from old custom, for on an Alaska coast there was formerly always plenty of driftwood.

In the spring, when the sun begins to thaw the snow, the Eskimo, if at all "primitive," leaves his house, regardless of whether it is an old type sod house

39

or a modern frame building, and lives in a tent for the summer. These were made of skins in the old days, but are now fashioned of canvas. Sophisticated people are beginning to live in houses the summer through, which, in the view of some authorities, is one reason for the heavy tuberculosis rate.

Eskimo houses around Point Barrow in the old days when driftwood was plentiful were made of wooden frames covered with earth to such a thickness that the houses were practically cold-proof. They were entered through a long alleyway by a door that was never closed, even on the coldest night of winter; the ventilating hole in the roof was open, too, assuring a constant circulation of air throughtout the house. A dwelling big enough for two average families (in one room) needed only three medium-sized seal-oil lamps to keep the temperature at 80° or 90° in the daytime, which dropped to 60° or 70° at night.

When the white man came, he built much larger, and incidentally draughtier, abodes whose flimsy walls admitted the cold more readily. These soon became the fashion, and the Eskimos did their best to copy them faithfully, with the result that they were unable to keep them as warm and cozy as their sod houses. Most of the driftwood along the beaches, which had been accumulating for generations of oil heated homes, now disappeared into the stoves that vainly tried to keep temperatures at the accustomed level.

The Eskimo's own type of house was infinitely better suited to the environment than the white man's, but the pull of fashion is strong. However, there are still many examples of the sod type of house at various points along the north coast.

The main plaza of the usual Eskimo village is the beach. All activities center along it and across it goes the village traffic. Highways to it are by water in summer and over ice in winter. It is from the beach that the hunters take off in their slender kayaks for seal, or a family starts off on a visit with all the children, dogs and gear piled into the family umiak.

The Eskimos hold views almost the opposite of ours about water and ice. To them ice is something friendly on which they walk and hunt and which protects them from the treacherous waters beneath. We usually think of the water as being safe, the ice as being treacherous.

Eskimos seldom learn to swim. The waters of the Arctic Ocean and Bering Sea are too cold, the mosquitoes are too many and too hungry. It is only

Above—*North of the Arctic Circle, beyond the tree line, Eskimos build their houses of driftwood and sod. Whale ribs are sometimes used instead of driftwood*
Below—*A sod roofed cache, the Eskimo's storehouse, is built high off the ground as a protection against curious wolves and bears*

the children in the hottest weather who take off their boots and socks and go wading in the shallow water off the beach. Even then they run in and run out without staying in the water more than a few moments.

The Eskimo hunting canoe, the kayak, is no doubt the most seaworthy craft of its size. The spruce driftwood frames are shaped by hand; the pieces, instead of being nailed together, are laced with wet rawhide, which draws tight as it dries. The covering is of sealskins and fully envelops the boat except for a round opening just large enough for a man.

In some districts the boat's one opening merely fits the hunter's body rather snugly so as to give water little opportunity to enter; or the opening may have a raised edge to which the Eskimo lashes the hem of his waterproof coat so that paddler and canoe are of one piece. Water is prevented from entering not merely through the manhole but also through the sleeves and neck of the coat, which are tightly lashed. This hooded raincoat is made from the intestines of the seal, which are dried and sewn together to make a translucent slicker which sheds water beautifully and looks somewhat like cellophane.

The kayak is about as steady on rough water as a man on a swaying tight rope. Its seaworthiness lies in the skill of the kayaker with his long double paddle, and in the boat and boatman being a single unit.

Two or several kayaks are sometimes lashed two together into rafts to insure stability especially when freighting or when spears are being thrown, the violent action of which might upset a single boat. They are sometimes built, though rarely, for two paddlers — this custom is practically confined to the Aleutian Islands.

Getting in and out of a kayak is a tricky business, and few white men can do it without falling into the water. It is accomplished by placing a pike pole or paddle across the opening of the boat, with the other end resting on ice or beach. When a steady balance has been achieved the kayaker ventures in or out. But don't try it on the basis of these instructions!

The pike pole mentioned above is a very useful implement. It is used for cutting ice, for pulling wounded game within reach and for propelling the kayak in shallow water.

Many tales are told of the swiftness of these wonderful boats and of Eskimo skill in handling them. When Sir Martin Frobisher met the Eskimos of what is now Baffin Island, during the reign of Queen Elizabeth, the natives

The beach of most Alaskan villages is the main thoroughfare in both summer and winter

saucily paddled right up to the British rowers; when pursued, by what were then about the finest oarsmen of Europe, they paddled easily away, leaving the English as if tied to a post. The splendid Indian canoemen of Ontario, who accompanied various early explorers and traders to northern Canada, were like Frobisher in their surprise and admiration. The kayak has, in fact, the lines of our modern racing shells.

When an Eskimo boy is about twelve years old, his father will begin to teach him the difficult technique of handling a kayak. Long before this time, probably when he was six or seven, he learned to use a gun. He has killed small game and, if lucky, a seal. He has gone out to his father's fox traps by dog team and perhaps made a short sledge trip or two by himself. But a kayak, unless expertly handled, is a very dangerous and tricky object. A boy has to be serious-minded and must work hard to master the art of handling this marvelous little craft, for a mishap may end in drowning.

Instructions usually begin in a quiet lagoon sheltered from the rough surf. The kayak is placed on the edge of the beach so that while it is standing in a few inches of water you can reach it from dry land. The father then gets into the kayak and explains how to hold and manipulate the paddle, demonstrating each step as he tells of it. When this is thoroughly understood, father and son change places and while his father holds on to the kayak, the boy goes through the motions of paddling. Step by step each maneuver is rehearsed and memorized before the boy takes to the water alone; and even then he is carefully watched and never goes far from shore to begin with. It takes years of practice to become an expert kayaker; but, once the skill is acquired, kayak and paddler become practically unsinkable.

Many accidents do occur in kayaks, but death will usually result not from the kayak overturning, because a good kayaker can right himself half a dozen times easily, but from the paddler getting a sudden cramp or being so fatigued from repeated capsizing that he is unable to continue paddling.

The kayak is used principally in fishing and hunting for ducks, seals and even for white whale.

While the small canoe or kayak is the greater marvel, nearly the same admiration is due the larger umiak. This is a kind of skin-covered dory which has long been known as one of the safest types, capable of long voyages in rough waters.

Learning to handle the tricky kayak. First the father demonstrates, then the
son practices while father holds the boat steady

Above—*Getting in or out of a kayak requires a good sense of balance. The paddler helps himself with his "gee" pole*
Below—*Pulling a kayak ashore*

An umiak can carry as many as sixty or seventy people. Here is one without its skin covering which shows the simple sturdy construction

The average umiak is thirty-five to forty feet long, big enough to carry two tons, and light enough for two men to carry. It is so strong and so fitted for rough handling that the Yankee whalers of northwestern Alaska in the latter part of the nineteenth century discarded the New Bedford whaleboat for the umiak in pursuing the bowhead whale. With a New Bedford whaleboat even a small fragment of floating ice will do great damage while an umiak going at the same speed will not be harmed at all. With a whaleboat it is as though the ice were struck by an egg shell; there is a crash and a dead stop. With a skinboat it is as if it were struck by a football; there is a thump and a rebound. If the umiak does suffer injury, it is merely a cracked rib that can be replaced, or a hole in the skin which can be patched with needle and thread.

Being light itself and having a flat bottom, an umiak draws only a few inches of water and can go in shallow places where an ordinary boat would be unable to navigate.

In summer time, in order to prevent the skin covering of the umiak from decaying, the boat must be taken out of the water and dried at least every four days — preferably every three. This is a simple matter. When a party camps for the night, the boat is taken out of the water and tilted on edge. If the weather is fair, the skins will be dry in the morning.

On land, as we have said, an important method of travel is still the dog team. A woman interested in learning "all" about the North once asked an Arctic explorer: "What exactly is an Eskimo dog?" His answer was: "Madam, an Eskimo dog, is any dog belonging to an Eskimo. You might as well ask 'What is a Pennsylvanian or a New York dog?' "

Undoubtedly once upon a time there was such a thing as a purebred Eskimo dog, but almost the first Europeans who came north brought with them dogs which were bred with Eskimo dogs. Today only two distinctions can be made. There are the small Siberian sled dogs, often pure white or black and white, sometimes with milky blue eyes, and the ordinary Eskimo dog which is really a mongrel and may be of almost any size or color. During the Gold Rush hundreds of dogs of various breeds were brought into the country, varying from St. Bernards to Newfoundlands and many Alaska Eskimo dogs show traces of those breeds.

The so-called pure-bred Husky dog is an artificial breed developed by white men after carefully breeding only dogs of a certain height, color and fur, which they had decided beforehand would be the ideal. These dogs, usually white and large, are commonly bred and trained in Maine and New Hampshire, and are shipped to the Arctic, to a wealthy miner perhaps, or the Antarctic where they have been used in exploration.

Some early fur traders sent out by the Hudson's Bay Company to Arctic Canada were cockney Englishmen who dropped and put in h's. They called Eskimos, Heskimos; an Eskimo dog was to them a Heskimo dog. This was soon shortened to Hesky, from which we get the term Husky dog.

The Eskimo sled dog is the unsung hero of many a dangerous journey. The close companionship and almost human understanding that a well treated team of dogs offers their master is beyond description. Hard working, willing and loyal whether well fed or half starved, they work all year round, in winter as sledge dogs and in summer as pack animals. If hunting is poor, the dogs are the first to have their rations cut, but many a starving dog has died in its traces, pulling with its last breath.

It will sometimes happen that snow will fall upon the coast ice and later

Eskimo boys are often given their own dogs to bring up and train

a shower of rain will form a skin of ice over the snow. On top of this will fall another cover of snow, but the thin layer of ice is left as a sort of roof over numerous cavities and soft places underneath, so that every few steps a dog may break through and get the sharp angular pieces of thin ice between his toes. Unless his feet are protected, after four or five days they will become sore and bleed until finally he will be unable to pull. To protect their pads from the cutting ice, little boots, usually of skin or canvas, are tied on to each foot. Skin boots last longer than canvas but care must be taken to keep the dog from eating his boots. Any dog with a normal appetite delights in eating seal, even in boot form.

Making trail over a new country, you may have to travel over this type of ice and snow. When the surface of the ice is very rough these boots will wear out fairly quickly and must be replaced. If you are good at multiplication it is easy to see that keeping a team of ten or twelve dogs, each with the usual four feet, well shod for a journey over this icy terrain would keep you pretty busy. On one expedition it was necessary for a party to travel two days and spend each third day making boots for the dogs.

Before the coming of the airplane and the caterpillar tractor, the dog sled was the only means of overland transportation in Alaska in winter time. As long as there is snow on the ground, and that may be for about seven months of the year, dog teams are used by trappers, hunters and mail carriers, not to mention the Eskimos.

The winter, when it is a little too dark to do any real hunting, is holiday time for the Eskimos and they spend a good deal of it visiting back and forth with friends. Their teams used to be small but now they average about thirteen dogs; the number may vary a good deal depending on the vicinity and the wealth of the owner. The lead dog is not necessarily the strongest in the team, but he is the most intelligent; it is he that interprets the driver's few commands. It is spirit that marks the lead dog, which is as likely to be a small female as a large male, and it is said that they are "born, not made." When a litter of pups are big enough, they are allowed to romp and run alongside a trained team. The pup that runs ahead and tries to stay in front is marked as a future leader. At least many Alaskans say it is as simple as that.

A good lead dog has a knack for scenting a trail made completely invisible by drifting snow, and many a lost sledder owes his life to a dog's way of guiding the team home.

You can always tell if a dog is loafing; his section of the towline will sag. If he does it often, one cure is placing him in front of an old veteran. Then he either pulls or gets nipped in the rear — if you credit a usual Alaskan report. Lazy dogs are rare; most of them are crazy about pulling, yelping excitedly when they are harnessed for a trip.

Sled dogs are fed only once a day, and their ration is usually a dried salmon, but they will eat almost anything they are used to. Dog fights often break out and must be stopped immediately, for they may result in the death or maiming of one or more dogs. For this reason they are seldom allowed to

Helping the dogs over a tough spot

run loose. After a day's work they are usually tied to a stake out of reach of each other. Sled dogs are workers primarily, not pets. For doing their particular job these tough but affectionate beasts are unsurpassed.

An Eskimo sled will carry from five hundred to a thousand pounds of load. An Eskimo, unless ill, will never ride on the sled. He is more likely to be up front giving the dogs a hand over a rough spot where the pulling is hard. If the sled is allowed to stop the runners will freeze to the snow, if the weather is really cold, in which case the sled is rocked loose with a gee pole.

White men have introduced some innovations, among them a kind of rude brake on the back of the sled. It will not stop a runaway team but is useful for slowing up the sled going down a hillside.

Many people are under the impression that an important reason why the Eskimos are able to survive in the Arctic and "endure the terrific cold" is that they harden themselves to it, and are better able to stand cold than white men. Few things are further from the truth. The Eskimos do not endure or suffer cold, they protect themselves from it. They wear clothing designed for warmth, lightness and comfort rather than looks. Their fur suits, skillfully made and practically cold proof, act somewhat on the same principle as a thermos bottle, keeping them warm as toast in the coldest weather. An Eskimo of northern Alaska wears in January a ten-pound suit in which he can sit in comfort on a cake of ice at 50° below zero, light a pipe in a leisurely way and smoke and chat indefinitely. Compare this with the average midwinter outfit of the New Yorker which weighs about fifteen pounds and would not keep him reasonably warm for fifteen minutes if he sat still at 15° below zero.

Eskimo cold weather dress consists of two suits of caribou, the inner one worn with the fur side inside and the outer with the fur side outside. Each suit is made up of coat, or attigi, and breeches, the latter tied about the waist with a drawstring, for there are no buttons or buttonholes on truly Eskimo clothing. Both undershirt and outer coat have hoods which expose the cheeks and forehead but protect the ears. Boots and mittens complete the outfit. Both inner and outer coat are usually worn loose; they are not tucked into the trousers. If the weather becomes cold or windy the belt is tied around the undercoat, preventing the cool air from coming up inside. If it becomes still colder, the belt is removed from around the undercoat and tied over the outer coat. By reversing method, if one becomes overheated through running or

*A young Point Hope Eskimo in his coat which has the skin side outside
and the fur side inside*

working, the belt is removed and cold air allowed to circulate over the warm body, or the outer coat may of course be removed entirely.

It is not enough to have suits of Eskimo fur clothing for protection from the cold, it is also necessary to know how to wear and care for them. Dry snow must be shaken carefully from them and hoar frost which forms on the inside must be removed before a warm house is entered; and most Eskimo houses are much hotter than ours in winter. A cotton snow shirt should be worn over the fur garments if it is snowing out to protect the fur, which must never be allowed to stay wet any length of time, for damp rots the skins.

Caribou is not the only fur used for skin clothing, but it is the best. Bear skin is used for trousers, sealskin for boots, white whale skins and walrus for boot soles. If nothing else is available, fox skins are used for coats. Seals are of course also used for boats, and bags are made from whole skins which are inflated and in which the Eskimos store seal oil or blubber.

The Eskimos formerly wore skin clothing in summer as well as in winter. Now they buy, either in villages or from traders, cotton cloth, which is of course much cooler than skin clothing and also offers better protection from sandflies and mosquitoes.

After the caribou skins have been dried and scraped they are soft and free from odors. Then the Eskimo women, wonderful seamstresses, fashion them into garments. Such skill as theirs is acquired only by years and generations of practice. With unbelievably careful stitching, Eskimo seamstresses make what is probably the only truly waterproof seam in the world. Our bootmakers do not think a seam can be waterproof in itself and usually rub oil or some sort of grease into the needle holes. If an Eskimo seamstress sees you rubbing oil on boots she has made she will feel insulted, thinking you suspect her seam needs greasing to cover defects of workmanship. When a woman finishes the last seam of a waterboot, for instance, she inflates it like a balloon, twists the mouth as a small boy does with a paper bag he is going to "bust," and waits for a few minutes to see if any air is escaping. She will hold the seam to her cheek to detect the escape of air, or near a steady lamp or candle flame to note the slightest flicker.

The skins are sewn with thread made of caribou sinew. Dampening a new pair of boots will make them even more waterproof, for the moisture causes the thread to swell, making it tighter than ever.

An Eskimo boy wearing his waterproof coat which lashes to the opening of his kayak

Those Eskimos who live near white settlements have naturally enough slowly acquired the fashion to wear white men's clothing; but as you get farther north toward Point Hope and Barrow you will find less and less imported clothing, more and more of the real Eskimo type.

One of the superstitions about the North that keeps popping up time and again is the notion that the best way to treat frostbite is to rub snow on it. Of course most of us now know that nothing could be more dangerous, since at 50° below zero the snow is about 80 degrees colder than the frozen part and freezes it deeper, acting practically like liquid air.

But many an ignorant miner, especially during the Gold Rush days, lost a leg or an arm because he believed this fable. The important thing in frostbite is to curtail the freezing, which is sensibly done by applying heat as quickly as possible.

The Eskimo's method of dealing with frostbite of the face is simple but effective. His coat is purposely made loose fitting, with the sleeves cut so that at any time the wearer can pull his arm in through the sleeve and carry his hand on his naked chest. The neck of the coat is also cut along ample lines. If an Eskimo finds that part of his face is beginning to freeze, he pulls his hand out of his sleeve, pushes it up through the neck of the coat and presses it for a moment on the freezing spot, which is soon thawed. Then he pulls his hand in upon his chest again. In this way he can walk all day in the worst weather, slightly freezing his face a dozen times or more but always thawing it before the freezing becomes deep.

With people who live in cold climates, whites who have learned the trick as well as Eskimos, to thaw your face becomes an unconscious gesture; you do it automatically and it doesn't even interrupt conversation between two people walking along the trail together, not as much as lighting a cigarette does here.

This slight freezing is perfectly harmless, about as serious as a slight sunburn and resembling it in that both sunburn and frostbite will make the skin peel if you let them get deep.

An important factor in keeping your face from freezing is to be clean shaven. If you wear a beard, the moisture of your breath congeals and sticks in it, forming a mask of ice which freezes faster than you can thaw it by the method just described. Eskimos have very sparse beards; what few hairs they have are usually plucked out as a precaution against frostbite.

Making a single long thong from a sealskin is an ancient Eskimo trick which requires two sets of hands and a sharp knife

Eskimo mothers carry their babies on their backs inside their coats, the child sitting pick-a-back fashion with its legs around the mother's waist. A belt to prevent it from slipping down is tied under the child in back, brought forward and tied in front over the mother's breast, as shown in the photograph on the opposite page. If the child is young, it is carried naked and is completely hidden from view inside the coat. As it gets older, and if the weather is mild, it is often carried with its head protruding from the top of the coat.

Frequently on a journey a naked child inside its mother's coat, warmed by her body heat, will become overheated and start to cry, whereupon its mother, regardless of how cold it is, and it may be 40 or 50 degrees below zero, will stop, spread a skin on the snow, untie her belt and let the child slip down. She places the naked child on the skin. At first the child grimaces and blinks. You may think this is because it has been shocked by the cold, but its mother will explain that the child makes those faces, because having come suddenly from the darkness inside the coat to the bright sunlight, it takes a moment or two to adjust its eyes to the change.

When it has become used to the light the child will smile and gurgle happily because the cold air feels *good* to its overheated body. But after a half or three quarters of a minute it will begin to hunch its little shoulders and pucker its face. The mother who has been watching the child carefully, recognizes this as a signal that it is sufficiently cooled off and slips it back under her coat, ties her belt and they continue on their way.

You may think this method of carrying and "air-cooling" a child is all very well for an Eskimo baby, that a white child would certainly never survive; but many white women, wives of missionaries and traders, have adopted this Eskimo method and all agree that for traveling in Arctic country it is much the easiest and most effective way. Their blondest children react to heat inside a fur coat and to air of 50° below zero exactly like the most pronouncedly brunette Eskimo baby.

Unless its parents are getting disagreeably civilized, an Eskimo child is never punished. You might suppose this due to the parents' fondness for their offspring, and fond they are. The common opinion of travelers is that few if any people in the world are so kind to and thoughtful of their children. Still the deep reason why children escape punishment is what Eskimos believe about the soul, or about what more or less corresponds to our idea of a soul.

According to their theory, a child is born with a soul and a body that are equally small and weak. It seems obvious to an Eskimo that the child would never get along if it did not have a more experienced and wiser soul to look after it; so the first thing the mother does after the child is born is to pronounce a spell and summon the spirit of some person who has recently died.

The Eskimos have no sex indication in their language. They have no pronouns like he or she in English; they have no sex inflexion for adjectives and nouns such as you find in Latin or in German. This may be part of the reason why it makes no difference in their thinking whether the spirit summoned is that of a man or woman. In some districts it ought to be the spirit of a near relative who recently died; in another district it may be the spirit of the last person who died, irrespective of relationship.

The Eskimo language has no distinction between the idea of a name and

A modern Alaskan Eskimo madonna and child

the idea of a soul; the word used for either in every Eskimo dialect from Greenland to Alaska and Siberia is *atka,* which most Europeans have translated as name. However, those who have a perfect understanding of the Eskimo language will soon notice that while name is a good translation of *atka* in some cases it is no translation at all in others. Nor will they discover upon cross questioning that an Eskimo has any ability to distinguish between the idea for a name and the idea for a soul. Of course we are speaking now of Eskimos not yet civilized.

It seems to be the Eskimo view of the spirits of the dead that they are strongest just after death and gradually become weaker; correspondingly it is their idea about the inborn soul of the child that it is weakest at birth and gradually becomes stronger. Accordingly, they are clear that when a child is very young its thinking is done for it exclusively by the soul of the dead person, the child's inborn soul having little or no control. So if a child cries for the scissors it is, in Eskimo opinion, the judgment of the guardian soul that the child ought to have the scissors.

This gives the parents two reasons for yielding. In the first place, who are they to think that they are wiser than the guardian spirit? And, anyhow, if they refused they would offend the guardian, which would thereupon leave the child. With nothing but its own incompetent soul to take care of it, the baby would suffer one misfortune after another. If it does not die it will be an imbecile, will develop a club foot, or at the very least will be sickly, disagreeable and unfortunate through life. It is especially deformities which Eskimos associate with an offended guardian spirit. If a man's ears stick out at the wrong angle or if his nose has a strange shape it is usual to hear people remark that his parents must have punished him when he was young.

Naturally there are halfway cases of offending the guardian spirit—it may not leave the child but may simply get disgruntled, not paying much attention to its job any more. It is really such cases which, in Eskimo thinking, account for physical deformity or bad health. Still, they resemble us in that their religious thinking is not always crystal clear. Ask one Eskimo what will happen if a guardian spirit is angered and he will tell you it goes away. Another will say that he has heard this about guardian spirits going away but that, in his own opinion, the child would not live in that case; so what usually happens, he thinks, is that the guardian spirit gets sulky or discouraged and does not protect the child adequately.

During the first few years of a child's life, you are distinctly speaking to the soul of the dead when you address the child. Therefore it is customary for those related to the dead to address a baby in terms of that relationship. For instance, if my grandmother's soul is in a small boy I will address him as grandmother, and I will say that I am bringing a present for my grandmother. This sounds particularly strange to us when a mother is talking to her own son and calls him grandmother or uncle, as the case may be.

While most Eskimos are now Christians, and not supposed to believe in all these spirits, the fact remains that to this day Eskimo children are practically never punished or forbidden anything.

We have been saying things every now and then which indicate that the language of the Eskimos is hard for us to learn. It may be almost the hardest language in the world. The active daily vocabulary runs above 10,000 words, most of which are either nouns or verbs; they get the adjective and adverb meanings by inflexion. The inflexion is so complicated that a single noun can be written in more than a thousand forms, each having a meaning of its own, while a verb can be written in still more different ways.

Then the structure of Eskimo is so different from what you are used to that you really have to learn not merely the words and their inflexions but also a new way of thinking. This will not be true, however, if you are a Finn, a Lapp or a Magyar, for those languages belong to the same family and, if you are in the habit of thinking in them, you will soon catch on to the Eskimo. If you do belong to one of those linguistic groups you may be able to learn Eskimo in a year, by steady application; if your mother tongue is English, French or Danish it will take you from three to five years of hard work unless you are a positive linguistic genius. We can do no more than begin to indicate the difficulty.

For instance, the average American who wants to learn the language seeks out an Eskimo who speaks English and, taking care not to be misunderstood, he will hold a knife in his hand and ask, "What is your word for knife?" The Eskimo will answer "savik;" "And what is your word for 'big'?" is the next question, whereupon the answer, in Colville River dialect, will be "angirok." "Now," thinks the white man, "I know how to say big knife;" but as a matter of fact he doesn't know at all, for the Eskimo does not say "big knife" by attaching the adjective for "big" to the word for "knife." He inflects the word and a big knife is not "savik angirok" or "angirok savik;" it is "savipuk."

61

For the inflexions take the word *iglu* which means a temporary or permanent shelter of any sort. *Iglupuk,* means a large house; *iglunguak,* a make-believe or playhouse; *iglorak,* a wooden house; *iglukuk,* a ruined house; *igluliak,* a house that someone built; *igluliapuk,* the house that the two of us built; *iglulik,* that which contains houses (used for instance for an island which is inhabited); *iglutun,* like a house, and so on for several hundred variants of the one word *iglu.*

The noun is simple compared with the verb. It is probable that no man has ever worked out the number of possible different ways in which a single Eskimo verb may be used, but one experienced Eskimo linguist has estimated it at a minimum of three thousand.

With even this beginning of an explanation it may no longer appear strange that some white men who have resided in the country twenty or thirty years, and are married to Eskimo women, cannot understand what their wives are saying when they talk to the children.

Because Eskimo has proved too difficult for all the neighbor peoples, whether forest Indians or whites, there has grown up a trade language, a jargon or pidgin, wherever an outside people has been in contact. The most elaborate of these jargons, almost deserving to be called a language, was developed in northeastern Alaska and northwestern Canada between the Eskimos and the Tinneh or Athapascans. The jargon used in most of Alaska was started by the early whalers who worked on the basis of another jargon which had been developed by American whalers up around Baffin Island and Hudson Bay. As spoken today, this jargon consists of between 300 and 500 Eskimo words, which are used uninflected and sometimes in very strange meanings. There are a few words from the Chinook jargon of Washington State and British Columbia, introduced by gold miners. A number of the words are from a jargon developed between whites and natives in the Hawaii Islands and some are from pidgin Chinese. Danish, French, Spanish and English have each a few representatives.

Naturally it is impossible to express any but the simplest ideas in 500 or 600 uninflected words, and this is no doubt the chief reason why so many white people in Alaska will tell you that the ideas of the Eskimos are very simple. They are in reality very complicated, although it is a complexity scarcely analogous to that of our mechanistic age and vocabulary. For a just comparison you have to go to the old literatures, to Homer and Isaiah, for instance.

It is one of the really enlightening misstatements to say that people like the Homeric Greeks, the biblical Jews, and the Eskimos, have many ideas about a few things, while we have a few ideas about many things.

One of the least changed things in Alaska is the Eskimo language, one of the most changed is their housekeeping. In the old days people sat on the floor or on the bed platform; today almost every household has chairs or stools. Most families possess several packing boxes which are used as reserve seats in case of visitors. Many Eskimos still prefer sitting on the floor, however.

Each family has some kind of a stove, about one third of them steel kitchen ranges imported from the States, of which they are very proud. Some of these stoves are costly modern affairs in bright enamel, with the usual dials and indicators, and represent an investment of several hundred dollars.

Nine out of ten households have sewing machines, thermos bottles, alarm clocks and flashlights. Some of the wealthy Eskimo families have electric plants, and their houses are wired for electricity. Practically every adult male has a telescope or field glass and a watch, and every family owns a primus stove, which is a gasoline stove operated on the forced air principle of a blow torch and is used for preparing the morning tea when it would take too long to make a fire, or more especially on the trail when a warm drink and sustaining food can be quickly prepared in a country where driftwood is scarce. It is taken along for cooking purposes on sea journeys in open skin boats, especially on the walrus hunts.

It has been said, with picturesque over-simplification, that the average household has a library of five books. The list usually includes a Sears Roebuck or Montgomery Ward catalogue, the Bible, a school reader, a hymnal and some aged novel. This is your modern Alaska Eskimo!

The Eskimos who live in villages where they attend church every Sunday are buried according to Christian practice, but in the more remote places the old method of making graves above ground, usually but not always out of reach of wild animals, still exists. The old custom of placing on the grave the dead man's household articles, which he is supposed to need in the spirit world is being discouraged, since it often works great hardship upon the survivors. Tools, guns, cooking utensils and even cabinet victrolas have been left to rust and deteriorate. The family does without but no doubt is compensated by the "satisfying feeling that their duty has been done," as Mr. Gilbert said it.

Before the white man's influence came to bear the Eskimos practiced a sort of communistic anarchy. If one member of the community caught a seal it was shared with those who had not been so lucky. If food was abundant, each member of the group was fed equally; and, by the same token, when food was scarce the group went equally hungry. There was no caste system and no difference in rank. Nobody held any office; there were no chiefs. No man could order another to do his bidding but men of judgment and skill were admired and consulted. There was absolute equality between men and women. A husband could not order his wife to do anything, or vice versa. All problems of these gentle people were discussed fairly and amicably. Their exuberant happiness seems to have been the result of perfect health and a fortunately natural attitude towards life and death.

How much of this is true today depends on how near the Eskimos are to the white man's influence. Those that live in or near the bigger cities have largely adopted the white man's customs. Food is no longer shared; in the Christian marriage ceremony women promise to obey their husbands, and jealousy, unknown among the primitive groups, is now common. But the farther north you go the more truly Eskimo become clothes, food, houses and ways of life.

The Arctic Eskimos, unlike the more southerly Eskimo and forest Indian, do not stand in awe of Western civilization. They know that in their country we are uncomfortable if not helpless without their clothing, their knowledge of the country, and without food shipped in to us from "outside." Unless he adopts Eskimo ways, a white man is a rather pathetic misfit in the Far North.

Ancient Eskimo graves

A typical Eskimo log cabin and garden at Unalakleet

CLOSE to 64° North Latitude on easternmost Norton Sound is a typical little Alaskan village. It is not the biggest village in Alaska nor the smallest; it is not the most civilized nor the most primitive; it is about as far from Seward on the south coast of Alaska as from northernmost Barrow. The weather is cold in winter, flower gardens blaze with color in summer. It is a nice average village. Unalakleet is how the whites pronounce and write its Eskimo name; it lies on the Unalakleet River about 150 miles southeast of Nome. Pronounce the name with the accent on the first and fourth syllables. We are going to use this place to get a close-up of village life in Alaska.

There was a native settlement at Unalakleet long before 1842, the year of the founding of a trading post by the Russians; but known history dates from that time. Some of its oldest Eskimo inhabitants can remember clearly when the United States purchased Alaska in 1867.

67

The shelving, sandy beach of Unalakleet has inland from it a ridge upon which the houses are built. Back of the ridge is a strip of low land parallel to the beach which the river overflows each spring. From it the land rises slowly and evenly to the Shaktoolik hills. North of the river these hills come down to the shore in high bluffs of sandstone.

The three most important white influences in the lives of the villagers are three people. In the order of their importance they are the missionary, the schoolteacher and the trading post operator.

Ernst B. Larsson, the present missionary, is a Swede like the founder of the mission, Axel E. Karlson. Karlson started the Swedish Evangelical Lutheran mission in 1887 and all the Eskimos are now Christians and very devout. The neat, white clapboard church, erected in 1901, holds as many as four hundred people when crowded. The attendance is good; about two hundred of the three hundred and twenty-eight inhabitants attend each Sunday, a much higher average than most towns of that size in the United States.

The Eskimos take their church going seriously. Every Sunday morning they walk solemnly in family groups which grow larger as they are joined by the families of other worshippers. Even in summer time, when people are a day's journey from town, fishing upstream, they stop on Friday evening and start back to town in good time so as not to miss the services on Sunday.

Aside from saving souls and directing the spiritual lives of the community, the church has made a great contribution to the people of Unalakleet by the introduction of agriculture among them. The early missionaries, and some of the schoolteachers, planted small gardens in order to have fresh vegetables for their personal needs. In 1923 the present missionary made a successful effort to interest the Eskimos. He obtained the necessary seed and carefully instructed the people in planting and cultivation methods, personally supervising most of the gardens the first year. He must have been very proud when in 1926, only three years later, the first commercial crop from local gardens was shipped out.

The main crop is potatoes. About twenty tons are grown each year, some families producing a thousand pounds each. They raise cabbage, cauliflower, rutabagas, turnips, carrots, beets, parsnips, lettuce, celery, onion, rhubarb, peas, radishes, swiss chard and spinach. About five or six thousand dollars worth of produce is grown each year and sold mainly to Nome and to commercial ships

Above—*Trooping to Church on Sunday morning*
Below—*The family starts for Church*

Above—*The Church*
Below—*Children as well as adults are attentive during the sermon*

An Eskimo woman prepares the vegetables she has grown in her garden

and Coast Guard Cutters that stop at the village. What is left over is stored in cellars or holes dug out beneath the floor of the house. Since the sub-soil is frozen permanently, this makes an excellent cold storage plant—it is easy to arrange your cellar so that it has a temperature just a little above freezing.

The vegetables attain great size. Some of the records are an eighteen-pound cabbage, a seven-pound cauliflower, a fourteen-pound rutabaga, a twelve-pound turnip, a three-pound head of lettuce, a two-pound potato. About fifty varieties of flowers are grown and more than a hundred species of wild flowers have been gathered in Unalakleet. The barren North, indeed!

In addition to the vegetable garden, almost every family now has a flower garden and lots of house plants indoors.

The growing season at Unalakleet is short if you reckon it by weeks, but you will see it is sufficiently long if you reckon it by hours of sunshine, for each

71

day of summer is long with many consecutive hours of sunshine. In June there is daylight for twenty-four hours, although the sun sets around 10:30 or 11:00 P.M. The plants grow according to the amount of sun they receive rather than the number of days they are in the ground, and this is believed to account for the size and goodness of the vegetables.

Garden produce is now standard in the diet among these Eskimos. Still, of course, to an Eskimo the most delicious food of all will always be meat of some kind, caribou, seal or fish.

All the schools in Alaska are under the supervision of the Bureau of Indian Affairs and the one at Unalakleet has three teachers. A man and his wife from the States, the regular teachers, are helped out by a native girl who was trained "outside." Only married couples are accepted for teaching positions in Alaska and when you realize that sometimes they are the only white persons in an isolated village it seems a sensible arrangement.

In 1940-41 our village school had ninety-eight pupils. They study until they reach the eighth grade. They are allowed to leave when they are sixteen years old, but so far those who have reached sixteen have reached the eighth grade as well. The children are taught reindeer habits, an important subject because each family owns about two hundred of these animals, reindeer tallying, gardening, skin sewing, boat and sled making and basketry. They study hygiene as well as reading and writing English. Most Unalakleet children are bilingual. They learn English quickly and speak it in school; at home Eskimo is the language used.

According to the teachers Eskimo children are bright and quick to learn, but are somewhat handicapped through being taught from the same text books that are used by schools in the States. Some of the ideas contained in these excellent books are completely foreign to the children. It is more than difficult for an Eskimo child who has never left his little isolated village on the Alaskan coast to visualize big cities, subways and skyscrapers. He may memorize dates and accounts of various wars and political turmoils of the United States but he seldom really understands them.

Charles Wesley Hawkesworth, who was schoolteacher at Point Barrow in the early years of the twentieth century, was convinced that Eskimo and white children were equally intelligent. One Eskimo pupil in particular, he assured a visitor, was exceptionally bright and thoroughly understood the

Above—*The schoolhouse at Unalakleet*
Below—*Children in school*

history of the American Revolution which he had been taught. His vistor was skeptical. Some years later Mr. Hawkesworth, who was one of the finest of the many open-minded teachers sent north by the Bureau of Education, met his visitor again and explained gleefully how wrong he had been. At the end of the term one of the questions in the final examination he put to his class in American history was: "What were the causes of the Revolutionary War?" The bright boy of the class wrote: "One of the causes of the Revolutionary War was that the British were so mean that they put tacks in the tea they sold to the colonists." Taxes were something a Barrow youngster could not grasp, but he had the necessary background, through dealing with the Yankee traders that followed the north coast of Alaska, for understanding food adulteration and commercial trickery. Unalakleet is nearer our civilization than Barrow and has more to do with it; perhaps by now they can get excited about taxation. Besides, the Hawkesworth story is from the time before the Eskimos had radios.

One of the women teachers at Unalakleet organized a rhythm band in which the children play drums, tambourines and two long sticks which they hit together to make a short accented note. It is her opinion that Eskimo children have a sharper sense of rhythm and are more musical than white children.

Schooling is finished for the youngsters at sixteen. The boys then go out with their fathers to hunt and trap, the girls take over part of the household duties and help with the family sewing. Lately, soon after graduation, a great many boys and girls have gone to nearby mining camps, working as laborers and cooks. Some of the adults go as well, the lure being good wages. They can earn as high as $10.00 per day, with free room and board—pretty good wages for a youngster of sixteen or seventeen.

The male member of the teaching couple in a small Alaskan town is usually the operator of the radio station, too, which is also under the direction of the Bureau of Indian Affairs. The radio has a thousand-mile radius and plays a most important part in the lives of Alaskans, as pointed out earlier in this book. In peace-time it is used to send government and personal messages, to report the weather and to instruct flyers making landings on strange airfields. Short wave sets are not provided by the government but most radio operators buy their own. About one hundred teachers in Alaska have short wave sets and communicate with each other constantly. Many a teacher has suddenly found himself drafted to perform a surgical operation and does so to instruction

74

Emil Fisher, the schoolteacher at Unalakleet, is also the radio operator

coming from the short wave radio set and sent by a doctor from the nearest hospital, which is sometimes hundreds of miles away. Scores of Quincy sore throats have been lanced and many a baby delivered by this method.

There are actually three stores or trading posts in Unalakleet; one big one and two small ones. Peter Bahl, a Norwegian who came to Alaska because of his knowledge of reindeer herding, runs one of the smaller ones; the other is run by the natives themselves. The establishment of Charles A. Traeger is the "main" store. Since 1913 it has been the principal trading center at Unalakleet. There has been competition from time to time. Once the Lomen Brothers, a large trading company, opened a competitive store, but Traeger has outlasted them all. He is a real institution in the town; like Charlie Brower at Barrow, he is much more than just a trader.

Charles A. Traeger, a typical sourdough or "oldtimer," at the window of his combination post office, trading post and home

Born in Kenton, Ohio, Traeger went north to St. Michael during the 1898 Gold Rush. He opened a store there; in 1913 he moved to Unalakleet and has been there ever since. The gold fever still possesses him and any spare cash he has goes to back white and native prospectors seeking the precious metal.

Like most of the rest of the west Alaska coast, Unalakleet is without a harbor and all supplies are brought ashore by lighter or small boats. Big ships must anchor about three miles offshore and barges, handled by tug boats, are used to land goods. Traeger owns the fleet of barges that bring the supplies ashore and does all the hauling and lightering of freight from commercial vessels for the village and for this whole section of the coast. From the middle of October to late April or early May no ships come to Unalakleet, for there is ice offshore.

The building that houses the trading post and Traeger's living quarters

Above—*The post office and main trading post at Unalakleet*
Below—*The inside of Traeger's trading post*

is one of the largest in Unalakleet and contains the post office as well. It is built of logs which are then covered with corrugated sheet iron, a common and effective method of building in the north. The window frames and doorways are painted white, giving it a fresh and tidy appearance.

Traeger is a kindly faced, middle-aged bachelor who lives alone, does his own cooking, and has a reputation for making excellent bread which he bakes in old coffee cans. A wind charger supplies current for his radio and electric lights in the house and store, both of which are completely wired. His living quarters have comfortable old-fashioned overstuffed furniture, silk-fringed lampshades, curtains and pictures, all of them imported at one time or another from the States. Traeger loves Alaska, which is one reason why he is perfectly content with his life there.

It is at Traeger's store that the Eskimos buy tea, sugar, coffee, coffee pots, flour, jello, canned goods, sun glasses, fox traps, hardware, tobacco, candy, chewing gum, blankets and American-made clothing.

Almost all the summer clothing of the villagers is made of imported materials. The girls wear cotton dresses just like the children in the States, and the boys wear denim overalls and shirts and woolen lumberjackets. However, nothing the white man has invented is any better for life in northern Alaska than their own Eskimo "kamiks" or waterproof boots called by the whites "mukluks." These are made of seal, whale or caribou and are still worn by most of the village, although some now own high rubber boots.

In winter time when the snow drifts to the very tops of some of the buildings, and there are only five or six hours of combined sunlight and twilight each day, the Eskimo fur coat which they call *attigi* but which the whites insist on calling by the non-Eskimo word "parka," is still the most efficient garment. The snow *attigi,* designed along Eskimo lines, is made of cotton material and is worn over the fur coat to protect it from rain and snow. These garments, together with an inner shirt of some light fur, such as fawn or muskrat, form a combination that makes temperatures of 40 or 50 below something to laugh at and enjoy.

Nils Boyne, a Laplander, is the government meteorologist at Unalakleet, which in simpler language means he keeps careful record of the weather. He also runs the only road house in the town. In a country where there is a hundred times more flying per capita than in the United States, weather is an

In wintertime huge snowdrifts form wherever a house or object faces the wind.

important subject and almost every town has a meteorologist who keeps records for the U. S. Weather Bureau. This is seldom a full-time job and the meteorologist is either the village schoolteacher or holds some other job. In the case of Unalakleet he is a tavern keeper.

A "road house" in Alaska is usually a log cabin with an extra room where travelers can spend the night and get three meals a day. The standard price almost all over the country, excepting the big towns, is one dollar for each item. A dollar for a room, a dollar for breakfast, a dollar for lunch and a dollar for dinner. This may sound excessive in the case of breakfast but when you consider it as four dollars a day for room and board it looks a little better. Almost all villages in Alaska have a road house. These vary greatly in size and in the quality of accommodations, but the prices are usually the same.

Until recently there were no pennies in use in Alaska, and even nickels and dimes were rarities. The cost of things was generally reckoned by dollars and

An Eskimo log cabin showing clearly the outer porch or vestibule where hunting gear, dog harness and fur clothing is deposited before entering the house proper

quarters; but more recently, especially in the big cities, smaller change is coming into use.

While the schoolhouse, church and mission at Unalakleet are built of white clapboard, the typical Eskimo house is a log cabin. Like most coastal towns on Bering Sea Unalakleet is on a prairie, but a few miles up the river are thick spruce forests which supply the lumber for these compact houses which follow a general pattern.

Each dwelling has a little entrance hall or vestibule which is built onto the main house as a separate wing. It is here in winter time that fur clothing is removed and any hoar frost that has gathered inside it carefully beaten out before entering the warm house where it would soon melt and wet the skins if it were not removed. Dog harness and hunting gear are usually left in this outer porch, the main purpose of which is to keep out cold and wind when the house is entered.

80

In cold countries the world over you find dwellings of earth supported by a wooden frame. White men have a tendency to build vertically the walls of these structures, and then they try to sod them up much as sod houses used to be built on the American prairie. However, a straight-out sod house, such as they used on the prairie, had the roof resting on the sod walls, so that the entire structure was tight; but when you sod up a log cabin, as whites in Alaska often do, the sod wall has a tendency to separate from the wooden wall, leaving a space between. This would be a fine thing if the space were completely enclosed, but it is usual with a white man's dwelling that the air gets into this open space. The whites try to get around this by building the sod wall carefully and of the best sod; if necessary they brace the walls from outside with leaning timbers intended to hold the sod against the wooden frame.

The Eskimos, and most non-white northerners, have a simpler and better way; they just see to it that the wooden frame of the wall leans in a little. Then, when they build the sod up against the wall, the sod will press against the wall through gravity. Indeed you do not need sod but can shovel up against your in-sloping wall almost any kind of earth; any kind will make a good wall excepting gravel, which is porous to the wind and must not be used.

The roofs of Eskimo houses, like those of most non-white northerners, are likely to be "cottage" style—sloping in from four sides instead of two. The windows used to be in the flat part of the roof, where the four sides do not quite come to an apex, and they used to be made of some transparent animal membrane—bladder, intestine, or thin skin prepared vellum style. Nowadays glass windows are ordinarily used, and they are more likely to be in the wall than in the roof.

Near each Unalakleet dwelling is a cache (pronounced cash) or storage house which is raised high off the ground as a protection against curious wolves or other marauding animals, and is entered by a ladder. Many of the roofs of these buildings are made of sod on which grass sprouts in summer, making the whole better for shedding water. Eskimos keep inside their houses only those things which are in actual use, so that reserves of food, dog feed, traps, furs, sleds and any extra furniture are stored in the cache.

Some years ago the Government introduced reindeer from Siberia to Alaska to give the Eskimos a supplementary means of livelihood and make them less dependent on white men for work and food. All the reindeer in

Alaska today are descended from the 1280 animals imported between 1892 and 1902 through efforts initiated by Dr. Sheldon Jackson and carried out largely by the Revenue Cutter service. In 1937 an Act of Congress provided that only natives (Eskimos and Aleuts chiefly) could own reindeer. The Government then purchased the herds owned by whites for redistribution to the natives. The reindeer is an ideal animal from the Eskimo viewpoint; its skin provides clothing and its meat food.

When reindeer were introduced at Unalakleet, eight Laplanders, skilled in herding methods and in the general care of reindeer, were imported from Lapland to instruct the Eskimos. These eight are now represented by about twenty, and their blond children go to school along with the Eskimos.

The Government gives each family about two hundred reindeer. A reindeer superintendent visits the village about once every three or four weeks to see that the herds are properly cared for. He also supervises the slaughtering of the animals, which takes place in the fall after the round-up, when the skins are still in fair condition for making into clothing—they are better for clothes earlier. The round-up time is a gay and happy time, which the Eskimos celebrate with games and contests. No part of the animal is wasted, even the sinew is used for thread in sewing the fur garments, and of course the delicious reindeer meat provides many a feast.

The villagers fish a great deal, for it takes a lot to feed seven or eight and ten to fifteen dogs. Salmon is the most abundant fish. Each summer, when they come up the river, the Eskimos pile their tents and fishing gear into their umiaks and paddle upstream. Each family goes to its favored spot, unloads, sets up a tent and catches salmon, usually between 3000 and 4000 in a season. A few are eaten fresh but most of them are dried.

As the fish are caught by the men, the women, with few but swift and sure motions of the ulu, or "women's knife," clean and split the fish into two fillets, which are held together by the tail. The head is cut off, the backbone and ribs removed, and the fish is ready to be dried.

Each log cabin at Unalakleet, along with its patch of vegetable and flower garden, has a rack for drying salmon. This looks something like the beginning of a cabin, without walls or floor, but with the long, thin trunks of young spruce trees in rows, and a sloped arrangement on top over which a tarpaulin can be thrown to protect the drying salmon from the rain. It takes about two weeks for the wind to dry the fish thoroughly, after which they are stored in the family cache and used as needed during the winter for food of both men and dogs.

Each hunter at Unalakleet manages to secure between fifteen and thirty seals in a season by the "auktok" method. Dressed in white suits for camouflage, they crawl out on the ice toward the seals, which come up to nap in the sun. The seal does not take long naps, however, for he is fearful of polar bears and more recently may have become wary of men. His naps commonly last forty or fifty seconds, or perhaps a minute. Between them he raises his head ten or fifteen inches from the ice and spends five to twenty seconds surveying the horizon; then he takes another snooze. The hunter, as he creeps up, must pretend he is another seal, or the seal will quickly slip back into the water. Fortunately the seal's eyesight is poor and he is easily deceived. As the seal sleeps the hunter advances; when the seal wakens the hunter lies motionless. But if the seal keeps watching him longer than a minute he must not remain motionless; the seal's suspicions will be aroused, for it is rare that a seal stays still that long. So after the one-minute period has elapsed the hunter must make seal-like motions, such as lifting his head ten or fifteen inches, looking around, and then dropping his head down on the ice again. Rolling about a little and flexing the knees, to imitate scratching with hind flippers, will also make an impression, which in eight cases out of ten will make a good hunter acceptable as a brother seal. Once a seal is convinced that the hunter is another seal, he stays convinced, and pays little attention to him thereafter, as a rule. The hunter thus gradually works up to shooting distance and the seal is his.

About forty white whales, or beluga, are caught each summer in Bering Sea by our villagers. They provide excellent food. The skin is used for boot soles, umiak coverings and for the best thongs and belts. The white whale is small compared to the hundred-and-ten-foot blue whale of the Antarctic and the ninety-foot Bowhead of the Arctic, but its advantage from the Eskimo point of view is that it is much easier to kill, since it is the size of a walrus or smaller. A single harpoon and float, and sometimes only a harpoon, are all that is needed to dispatch the animal. In recent years they have been shot with rifles, but since they usually sink they must be harpooned practically at the same time, so the rifle is no great advantage.

83

An Eskimo woman's knife is called an ulu *and is used for a hundred different purposes. Here it takes the place of knife, fork and dish in the eating of* muktuk, *or raw white whale skin which has some of the blubber attached*

A favorite dish of all Eskimos and of many resident whites is maktak (sometimes written muktuk). This is the skin of a whale so removed that a quarter inch or half inch of blubber remains attached to the inner side. For eating, this is cut into strips. Many prefer it raw, cutting the maktak into cubes or domino-shaped pieces like lumps of sugar. If your teeth are good it is only pleasantly tough. The blubber, if fresh, has a taste resembling cow's cream; the skin part has a mild slightly walnutty flavor. About half the time the dish is eaten boiled, whereupon the blubber has about the taste that you are familiar with when you come upon a fat piece in a lamb stew; the skin retains its walnutty flavor.

The white settlers, especially the real old timers, make from maktak two

kinds of pickles. One sort is made like pickled pig's feet, and gives about the same effect; another is a spiced pickle for which Charlie Brower, most famous of all Alaskans, is additionally famous. Practically every newcomer who tries his pickles is a convert from that moment; some become addicts.

In winter, most Eskimos run trap lines some distance from the village. Each, by common consent, has a general district respected by others where he sets his traps for fox, beaver, mink and land otter. Frequent sledge trips are made to the trap lines and the pelts are exchanged at the trading posts for guns, ammunition, food and other necessities. In the spring youngsters and their grandmothers go out on the hills to trap for ground squirrels, which are made into fancy dress coats.

Almost every family in Unalakleet, and there are about fifty-five, has a team of dogs which average about thirteen in number. A little low log cabin is usually built for them as shelter in the cold weather, although they are perfectly capable of staying outdoors during the coldest season. The villagers, like most Alaskans, nowadays hitch their dogs two by two in a long line, with a single lead dog at the head, which is why Alaska dog teams are usually counted in odd numbers—nine, eleven, thirteen, fifteen.

Most of us have heard that one of the strange things about the Eskimos is that instead of kissing they rub noses. Now it is true that some Eskimos rub noses, but it is untrue that it takes the place of kissing. It is a gesture of affection, used chiefly between older women and very young children or between a mother and her new-born babe; it is never used between men and women as a part of courtship in the way pretended by some writers—except in movies, where "Eskimo" actors (usually Chinese, born in California) are made to do it for the edification of the theatre public.

Until the spring of 1940 there was a government nurse who tended the sick in the village. When she left, her place was taken by an Eskimo woman, Thora Sussick, who so far has successfully brought more than forty new babies safely into the world. The average number of children per family is five or six at Unalakleet, but there are as many as ten in some.

The village recently voted almost unanimously favoring a petition which decrees that no one shall be allowed a liquor license in the village and that no liquor of any kind be sold. This is a blessing, for like many of our diseases, the Eskimos have no inherited immunity to liquor and a very little will make them roaring drunk and completely unlike their usual quiet, jolly selves.

Remote as it is, a surprising number of people pass through Unalakleet every year. It may be scientists on their way northward, or into the interior; or prospectors on their way to inspect a new site suspected of harboring precious metals. A politician stops to make friends and store up good will for future elections. Aviators make emergency or deliberate landings, bringing people and supplies in and perhaps taking a sick Eskimo back to a hospital. Trappers, tourists, explorers, doctors and dentists make at least one yearly visit. Supply ships bring stock for the trading post and take back soft and precious furs. Government boats stop to pick up fresh vegetables and drop a government official; and Coast Guard cutters restock with fresh meat and vegetables.

Eskimos do rub noses! But it is an affectionate gesture used between very young children and older women

To the old-timer nothing brings home the meaning of the phrase "the blessings of civilization" like seeing a dentist in an Eskimo community. Today he is welcome and desperately needed; fifty years ago, or at most seventy-five, he would have been a curiosity and an incongruity, for then literally every person in a community like that of Unalakleet had perfect teeth, in the sense that no one had cavities, there was no dental caries. Today they have teeth about as bad as you would expect in New York or London.

That decay of the teeth was formerly unknown does not rest merely on what the old Eskimos tell you and upon what was written by travelers of fifty and a hundred years ago. For explorers have brought back to museums hundreds of skulls that had belonged to men, women and children who died before European foods came in. A check-up on more than 800 of these skulls, deposited in various museums, showed no cavity in any tooth. The investigators did find, true enough, one skull in a collection at the American Museum of Natural History of New York which had decayed teeth, but it turned out that the specimen had been misplaced—an India ink mark on it showed that it was not an Eskimo skull but one of a forest Indian from up the Yukon, where vegetables were eaten to a certain extent.

For this appears to be the key: Even so-called primitive people have tooth decay if their diet contains any considerable amount of food that comes from the vegetable kingdom. The like is true of European skulls, no matter how ancient. The mummies of Egypt have cavities in the teeth though they are from many thousands of years ago, for the Nile River people were to a large extent herbivorous.

There are some who believe that sugar is the chief enemy of the teeth, and that may well be so; at least, two things have been happening together among Europeans during the last few hundred years, a steady increase in the use of sugar and a steady decrease in the soundness of the teeth. However, no sugar was in use, as such, among the forest Indians of the United States in pre-Columbian times, and still their skulls show considerable tooth decay. They ate, of course, a good deal of things like corn, potatoes, beans and squash.

It was one of the marvels of the early travelers in Alaska to see the Eskimos using their mouths as we use such tools as vises and claw hammers. They were able to do it because every tooth was sound. We find in the old skeletons from Alaska a number of broken teeth, for not even the soundest can stand everything. The point is that even the broken teeth did not decay.

Nalukataktut is a kind of blanket tossing game played at holiday time. A walrus hide is used instead of a blanket and the tossing is accompanied by singing and drum playing

Around 1910 it was common in Alaska to meet people who could tell you almost to the year when they first heard of tooth decay and toothache. It would seem, from what they said, that a grown person might begin to feel the effect of the white man's diet in somewhere between four and ten years. Children who started using our food during the first few years of life would have decayed milk teeth, followed by decay in the second set of teeth.

The schools of Unalakleet, like others throughout Alaska, teach children to brush their teeth, with other devices for keeping the teeth and mouth clean. The success of that method of preventing tooth decay has been about the same in Alaska as farther south.

The Eskimos dearly love celebrations of every kind. New Year's Day and the Fourth of July are festivals with shooting contests and tests of strength.

Prizes are offered for the finest vegetables and the most skillful examples of sewing.

Under the supervision of the teacher the school often has game nights in which young and old participate, and as said reindeer round-up time is also holiday time. Many of the Eskimos have victrolas and records. From phonograph and radio they have developed a particular fondness for mountaineer and cowboy ballads, their favorite singers being Gene Autry and Bing Crosby. They also have records of popular music, with the result that when a group of white people stay in the village modern dances have been held and the Eskimos are learning the new steps. They have also made up a string band which entertains on special occasions.

Eskimos, young and old, dearly love to play marbles, chew gum, smoke, and eat candy. In their jolly fashion they make each visit of a newcomer an excuse for a party. They play cards a good deal and have become expert gamers, as the schoolteacher and several visitors have found out. Rummy and double solitaire are their favorite games; in both cards and checkers they usually beat white men.

In the evening the people visit each other back and forth. A glass of blueberry juice, the berries for which they gather each summer, is the usual offering to a guest.

Happy by nature, Unalakleet Eskimos find pleasure in almost all their activities, whether it be gardening, hunting, visiting or playing.

IN JULY 1942 the Japanese bombed Dutch Harbor and made landings on Kiska, Agattu and Attu, three of the Aleutian Islands. In the United States long unused maps of Alaska came out, and the Aleutian Islands, hitherto little known, began to take on personality and importance to the average citizen. How far were these islands from the mainland? How near to Japan? Was it really true that the fog was so thick as to make observation and attack almost impossible for our planes during part of the year?

The whole population of the Pribilof Islands, north of the Aleutians, numbering about four hundred, was evacuated to Admiralty Island in southeastern Alaska. The Aleut refugees at first complained a great deal about the heat, for the temperature on Admiralty Island rises to around 80 degrees in summertime, while on the Pribilofs it seldom goes above 64 degrees. The natives of Atka Island were also evacuated to Admiralty Island, where, homesick and bewildered, they are trying with but little success to understand Japan's attack and the reason

91

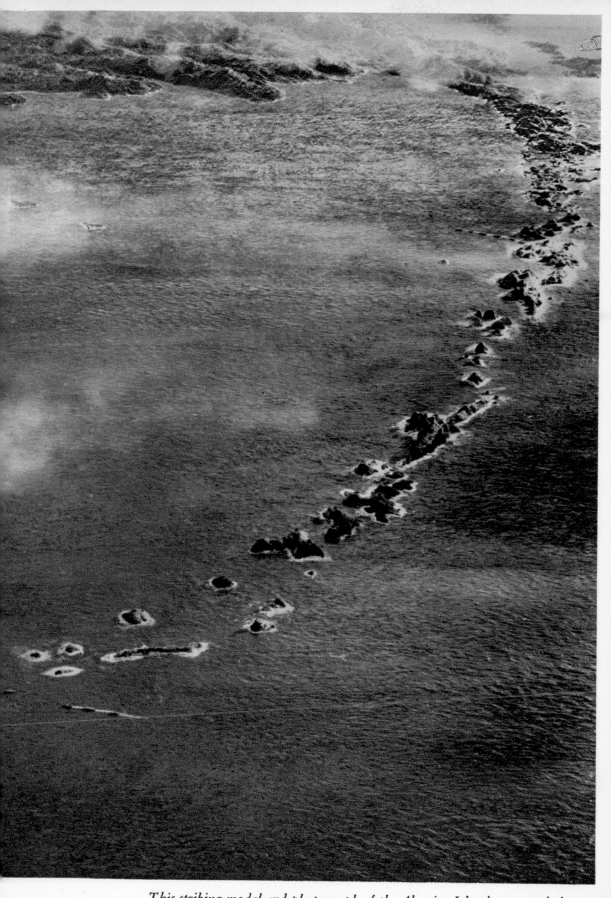

This striking model and photograph of the Aleutian Islands was made by Norman Bel Geddes for Life Magazine

for their transportation from their beloved country. They who had never seen a tree before are now in the midst of a towering spruce forest, which they by no means appreciate. There, beside Alaska's Inland Passage, which we think so beautiful, they will stay for the duration of the war—perhaps long enough so they will get used to the climate and the trees, beginning to agree with us about the beauty of the Passage.

For us, who look on from a distance and wonder, here are some of the answers to our questions about the Aleutian Islands, and those other islands which lie near them.

THE ALEUTIANS

The Aleutians are the tops of a partially submerged mountain chain which once linked Asia and America. No one knows exactly how many islands there are in the group; estimates have varied from sixty-two to as much as one hundred and fifty. They are divided and sub-divided into groups, the most important of which are the Fox Islands, which include the islands westward from Unalaska, the Andreanof Islands, the Rat Islands and the Near Islands.

The Aleutians are among the foggiest places in the world. When cold air meets warm air, the mingling produces fog. South of the Aleutians are the warm waters of the Pacific, with its Japan Current; north of them are the icy waters of Arctic Bering. The result in the air above the water is often what the aviators call "pea soup" fog.

Indeed the Aleutian Islands are said to have only two seasons, a rainy, foggy and cool summer and a comparatively mild, somewhat more clear winter. The most striking feature about weather in the Bering Sea area is its great uncertainty. Good weather is rare and brief; the wind shifts direction quickly.

The Aleutians, and many other coasts of Alaska, have williwaws. These are violent puffs of wind that sweep down from the mountain slopes. You meet them coasting along shore, and in many harbors. The danger to a vessel at anchor lies in their suddenness and in the radical changes in the direction of successive gusts. A vessel will toss wildly and is likely to break out her anchor. Williwaws strike terror into the hearts of sailors, particularly those on small sailing boats which are liable to capsize. A man cannot stand against a violent williwaw.

The innumerable passes between the islands have strong and treacherous tidal currents. Little accurate information has been published about them and they have earned the reputation of being dangerous. So they are, to the uninitiated.

During the years 1930-40 while local distrust of the Japanese was growing, Alaskans commonly told you that the people who really *knew* the Aleutians were the Japanese, whose fishing boats have been skirting the islands, coming in as close as they dared and often landing on the lonelier ones, especially since 1920. No doubt they took soundings and made maps. So little was known of some of the islands that, it was said, old Russian sailing charts dating from before the Purchase of Alaska were still in use as late as 1940.

However, these Alaska views, though emphatically written and spoken, were somewhat exaggerated. Coast Guard vessels kept plying the island waters, making valuable notes and taking photographs. Towards 1940, when the Alaska distrust of the Japanese began to be shared at Washington, surveying was intensified along all Alaska shores except the northern, and was no longer done by the Coast Guard, but was shared in by the Navy (of which the Coast Guard is not a part except in time of war) and by the Coast and Geodetic Survey.

Contrary to the usual belief of the outside world, the channels between islands are free of ice throughout the year; ice never forms except on the inner bays. The ocean is equally free of ice north and south of the chain. If you spent ten years on the top of the highest of the Aleutians with a telescope looking northward into the Bering Sea you would never see a cake of ice. It is only when you get east towards Bristol Bay that floes would begin to appear in the north.

The mild, intelligent natives who normally inhabit these far away islands, the Aleuts, are closely related to the Eskimos in language and culture. Like the rest of the Indians of the New World they are of what we usually call mongol type. Like the coastal Eskimos of the mainland, they subsist chiefly on the products of the sea; their boats and implements are similar.

About a hundred and fifty years ago the first Russian traders landed on the islands. They were greeted by the friendly Aleuts in a kindly and hospitable manner of which the Russians were quick to take advantage, after a pattern that has been too common when European pioneers dealt with the natives of the Americas. A series of cruelties, thefts and brutal killings marked the advance of the fur hungry traders as they pushed on from island to island, slowly changing the surviving Aleuts into an embittered, fierce, war-like people. Under the Royal Monopoly called the Russian America Company they were forced into a state of semi-slavery as hunters, chiefly of the sea otter. The hunters and the hunted alike decreasing rapidly as a result.

In the wake of the Russian traders came the Greek Orthodox missionaries who converted the people.

While the lure of rich furs brought many to the Aleutians one man whose name shines brightly in Alaskan history came because of his devotion to an ideal.

Father John Popov Veniaminov was not the first missionary but he was the first to learn the language and to take a real interest in the culture and human welfare of the inhabitants. In a native skin-covered kayak he paddled from island to island talking with the Aleuts about their traditions and customs and living with them in their half-underground barabaras or sod houses.

Having mastered the difficult language, he reduced it to writing. He translated into Aleut the catechism and the Gospel of St. Matthew, and opened a school in Unalaska where he taught the children to read and write. His grammar of the Aleutian language is still the standard, in fact the only good work on the subject. The first translation of it has recently been made by Mr. R. H. Geoghegan of Fairbanks and its publication is being considered.

Father Veniaminov's careful description of the Aleuts and their customs is still used by anthropologists.

Under the name of Innocent, Father Veniaminov later became Archbishop of Kamchatka, the Kuriles and the Aleutian Islands. He finally achieved the highest office of his church and became Metropolitan of Moscow.

Many of the Russian traders settled in the Aleutians and married Aleut girls, so that most of the present day Aleuts have a good measure of Russian blood. Before the war about four thousand Aleuts, peace loving and cheerful because the early brutalities had been forgotten, inhabited the islands and parts of the Alaska Peninsula. In July, 1942, however, all residents of the Aleutians not actively connected with the Army or Navy were evacuated to southeastern Alaska for the duration of the war.

Except for some Sitka spruce planted in Unalaska, the entire chain of islands is treeless. Willow shrubs grow only in the easternmost part; dwarf shrubs and herbs are found in the more westerly islands. There are many islands in the group suitable for animal husbandry. In some places the thick grass reaches a height of four feet.

No large land animals inhabit the Aleutians except where ordinary domestic livestock or reindeer have been introduced. There are sheep and reindeer on

Umnak, reindeer on Attu and Atka, cattle on Chirikoff and Chernofsky, cattle and sheep on Unalaska, sheep on Kashega.

Linked with the grazing industry are the problems of transportation, maintenance and labor. The islands are about one thousand miles from the nearest large U.S. port, Seattle, and steamers do not land at all places where grazing areas are available. Commercial steamship lines call at Dutch Harbor and Unalaska normally, but nowhere else in the chain. Haymaking is difficult, for the season is short and rainy for curing the hay. The air is so moist that hay which was dry when shipped will absorb sufficient moisture to heat and become mouldy when it is placed under shelter in the open. Except in the western part of Unalaska and Umnak, where snow seldom remains on the ground longer than a few hours, stock must be maintained by feeding during February, March and April. There is no white labor and the natives do not always understand our strange ways, or we theirs, so that trouble often results.

Many of the islands are now used as fox farms, some of which are owned by Aleuts. A keeper lives on the island throughout the year in some cases, in others foxes run wild and are trapped about every two years.

Sailing westward from the Alaska Peninsula you would pass Unimak Island, the first of the Aleutian chain, which is separated from the peninsula by the very narrow Isanotski Strait, or False Pass. This is the largest of the eastern Aleutians and the home of the magnificent Shishaldin Volcano, locally referred to as Smoking Moses. Several times in recent years Shishaldin, which rises majestically for almost ten thousand feet, has been in eruption; and faint wreaths of smoke and vapor still drift from its summit, making a striking picture, for the volcano is largely snow-clad. Pogromni Volcano, whose Russian name means "desolation," is a smaller conical peak near the western end of the island, also snow covered.

Westward of Unimak is the Krenitzin Group, the largest member of which is Akutan Island. There was a native village of the same name here. Across the harbor was a whaling station, maintained by the American Pacific Whaling Company, which caught two hundred or more whales in a good season and refined the oil on the island to be used as a cooking oil, as a fine lubricating oil for airplane motors, and for better grades of toilet soap.

Unalaska, the next large island, is mountainous. During the greater part

97

of the year its higher elevations are snow-covered. Makushin Volcano, almost six thousand feet, is the highest point on the island. Unalaska Bay, on the northern shore and open to Bering Sea, is one of the most important bays in western Alaska. It contains the important harbors of Iliuliuk Bay, Unalaska Harbor and Dutch Harbor.

The port of Unalaska, founded by Solovief between 1760 and 1770 as a fur trading station, was opened as a U.S. Customs port only in 1891, during the Klondike Gold Rush, although it had been much used by American and Russian vessels for many years prior to that date. It is a half-way station for ships plying between Seattle and Nome; and food and fuel supplies were stored here for emergency uses. With the passing of the Gold Rush and the decline of bowhead whaling, which ceased around 1906, the village has declined. Just prior to the war its importance lay chiefly in that it was headquarters for the U.S. Coast Guard fleet which patrolled Bering Sea from April to September. Unalaska had an excellent Native School, maintained by the Methodist Mission, a well equipped hospital which was operated by the Bureau of Indian Affairs, and some herring, halibut and cod fisheries which were operated by the natives. The Greek Orthodox church building in Unalaska is one of the largest of Alaskan churches, second only to the one at Sitka, the old Russian capital.

On January 15, 1942, the port of Unalaska was closed to shipping. No foreign ships were allowed to enter the harbor; even U.S. ships thereafter had to obtain special permission and to post a bond before being allowed to enter.

Dutch Harbor, in Unalaska Bay, was once a flourishing settlement and the capital of the fur sealing industry. It deteriorated steadily until a few years ago the total population was only seventeen. Just before the war the U.S. Navy built a base here, the size of which is a military secret; but the village has undoubtedly expanded considerably. In 1942 Dutch Harbor was the scene of the first Japanese attack upon North America.

Westward about sixty miles from Unalaska is volcanic Bogoslof Island, the mystery land of Bering Sea. It has been nicknamed the Disappearing Island and there have been many conflicting reports about it.

An island about the size and position of Bogoslof was first reported in 1768 by Krenitzin and Levashef, and then by Captain Cook in 1778. Father Veniaminov, the beloved Russian missionary to the Aleutian Islands, reported that in

98

Bogoslof is an active volcano in Bering Sea, just north of the Aleutians

1796 it rose from the sea accompanied by earthquake, shooting flames and columns of smoke.

Most people think that every now and then Bogoslof has disappeared, or at last has sunk so low that it was no more than insignificant peaks or islets. However, some officers of the Coast Guard have said that many of the disappearance reports are likely the result either of bad navigation on the part of the reporters or because they were using an incorrect chart. For there have been maps placing the island so far from its true position that if you were on the marked spot you would not be able to see the real island even if it were then as big as it ever was. But it is not denied by those who hold this view that Bogoslof has been changing now and then both in shape and size.

In 1937 this uninhabited island was clearly divided into two parts, the main island and a smaller one. The shape of the smaller, called Fire Island, was like that of a medieval castle with three towers. The larger island, of which Castle Peak is the highest part, gives the impression that the whole sea bed has been pushed up bodily, with an enormous evenly-applied pressure.

Bogoslof has been reported to be smoking and dotted with hot springs in which you could boil eggs, and then again to be completely dead and cold. Numerous sea lions breed on the island and, though they disappear during eruptions, bulls, cows and pups come back again when all is quiet. Sea gulls and horned puffins also nest and breed on the rocky cliffs.

Male fur seal

Australian sheep at Unalaska

When last seen, steam, with a trace of sulphur fumes were issuing gently from the cracks near the top of the volcano. In some places the rock felt warm to the touch.

Umnak Island, separated from Unalaska by Umnak Pass, is about seventy miles long and is the third largest island in the Aleutians. A herd of fifteen thousand sheep owned by the Aleutian Livestock Company grazed on the island before the attack on Dutch Harbor. There was a settlement on Umnak called both Umnak and Nikolski, which had the usual church, store and school.

Next in line, and westward of small Seguam Island, is the Andreanof Group, about half a dozen large and numerous smaller islands. Amlia, the most easterly, is about forty miles long and very narrow, with a chain of sharp peaks running throughout its length.

Atka Island, the largest of the Andreanof Group, contains Korovin Volcano, which rises almost five thousand feet.

The native Aleut women on Atka and on Attu, the westernmost Aleutian island, were famous for their exquisite baskets which they made of beach grass and which often took two or more years to complete. The grass was gathered in the fall when it was turning brown, split into thin strands and bleached. Then the long and tedious process of weaving began, the weaver keeping the grass moist in a damp cloth. With the grass were woven threads of colored embroidery silk to make a watertight vessel, which was decorated with native Aleut designs. These beautiful baskets are highly prized by collectors and have brought as much as one hundred dollars each. In 1942, as we have read, these natives had to leave their homes for a place of greater safety.

The rest of the Andreanof Islands are relatively unimportant, but they have strange and wonderfully sounding names like Koniuji, Igitkin, Kanaga, Tanaga, Kavalga, Unalga, Ulak and Ilak.

The Rat Islands come next. Simisopochnoi Island, also called Island of the Seven Mountains, has a sea lion rookery on it. The position of the small group formed by Little Sitkin, Chugul, Davidof and Khwostof has been disputed. It will not be known exactly until the maps of the recent government surveys are published. Kiska Island, another of this group, has more level ground than most of the Aleutians and about the best harbor in this part of the world. It is one of the three islands occupied by the Japanese in 1942, soon after the attack on Dutch Harbor.

We come to the end of the chain as we reach the Near Islands, so called because they are so near the Asiatic Mainland, Siberia. They are two, Agattu and the westernmost, Attu. There was an Aleut village on Attu, which used to be visited once a year by a Coast Guard vessel. These islands were occupied by the Japanese troops at the same time as Kiska.

* * *

So much for the Aleutians. There are other islands, besides the Diomedes mentioned in the first chapter, which stretch out into the Bering Sea. Any one of them may at any time during the war appear suddenly in the spotlight, so it is well to know something about them. Look on the map and you will see the groups that lie north from the Aleutians in this order:

The Pribilof Islands
Nunivak Island
The St. Matthew Islands
St. Lawrence Island
King Island
and
Little Diomede Island

THE PRIBILOF ISLANDS, HOME OF THE FUR SEALS

Two hundred and fourteen miles north of the nearest land are the four islands that make up the Pribilof Group: St. Paul, St. George and the two small, uninhabited islands, Otter and Walrus. They are frequently referred to as the Seal Islands. There live the fur seals that are probably the only aquatic animals in the world that have the honor of being escorted to their summer home by the U.S. Coast Guard, which protects them from illegal hunters at sea.

The islands are named after their discoverer Gerassim Pribilof, a Russian. In 1786, while sailing among the Aleutians, he noticed the migrating fur seals and decided to follow them to their breeding grounds, the location of which had long been a mystery. He set sail northward to find the land he believed must exist and was lucky enough to take an almost direct route. Landing on June 12, 1786, he named the island on which he stood, St. George, after his ship. So foggy are these islands that it was a year before St. Paul, the larger island, was sighted although it is only forty miles away.

Ever since then the Pribilofs have been famous as the summer home of the fur seal and the largest seal rookery, or breeding place in the world. Volcanic in origin, they are enveloped by fog nine days out of ten in summer. There are only two seasons on the islands, the foggy wet summer and the dry windy winter. The damp summer climate is perfectly adapted to the needs of the breeding fur seal.

Neither of the two larger islands has any harbor, and navigation is generally dangerous. The group is near the southern limit for scattered ice in Bering Sea; detached pieces may be seen from their shores between February and May.

Once Pribilof had discovered the breeding place of the fur seal, first cousin to the sea lion, wholesale slaughter began. It has been estimated that from 1799 to 1834, two million animals were killed. From 1835 until our Purchase of Alaska, in order to preserve the diminishing herds, it was forbidden to kill all female seals.

Later, when the route of the seals' annual migration, which had long been unknown, was solved, came pelagic sealing, or the taking of the seals at sea. Sailing schooners would follow the herds from the Oregon coast to the Seal Islands, killing as they went. Then they would lie off the islands waiting for the mothers as they went out to sea to secure food for their young. This caused a rapid decrease of the herds. In an effort to stop the slaughter, our Government called conferences and passed laws, but to no avail. The U.S. laws drove the sealing boats under the Canadian flag, and they managed to get many a seal despite the revenue cutters that patrolled the sea.

By 1910 the two million animals had decreased to one hundred and twenty-five thousand. In that year the Government took charge of the rookeries and negotiated a treaty with Great Britain, Japan and Russia, by which pelagic sealing was discontinued. Since then, through care and scientific management, the herd has increased steadily until now it is estimated at two million five hundred thousand. Each year a small percentage of three-year-old males are killed. In 1939, these amounted to sixty thousand. The skins are then sold at fur auctions and made up into the lovely soft brown fur coats that you see advertised for milady as "Genuine Alaska Seal."

In 1940 Japan denounced the treaty and proclaimed her sailors would take the seals wherever and whenever they could be found.

The names applied to members of the seal herd are curious. The mature male is called a "bull," his wife a "cow" and their youngsters "pups." The bull and his family constitute a "harem" and a congregation of harems is a "rookery." The three-year-old males are called "bachelors" and it is these that are killed each year.

The seals live from twelve to fifteen years and the male usually weighs four or five times as much as the female. After she is three years old the cow gives birth to one pup annually, a day or two after her arrival on the island. The mother goes to sea in search of food for her offspring and may travel a long distance, remaining away for two days; but it is said that, after a bit of looking, she can always spot her own child among the thousands on the beach.

Female Fur Seal

Although the Pribilofs are treeless, they are covered in summertime with deep green and yellow-green vegetation. Many a visitor has been pleasantly surprised when the fog has lifted to disclose the islands, bright with the color of flowering plants, luxuriant grasses and moss. During the breeding season millions of sea birds make their summer home on Otter and Walrus Islands, almost covering them.

There were two modern thriving Eskimo villages on St. Paul and St. George complete with schools, hospital and recreation halls, and it was from these villages as well as the Aleutian Islands that puzzled and dismayed natives were evacuated to Admiralty Island.

Nunivak Island, the second largest in Bering Sea, off the route of travel and rarely visited, is the scene of the Department of Agriculture's interesting experiments with musk oxen and reindeer. Over fifty miles long and fogbound most of the time, the island is separated from the mainland by Etolin Strait.

The two hundred Eskimos who like on Nunivak are considered among the most primitive in 'Alaska. As late as 1926 they were still wearing the lip, ear and nose ornaments of beads and walrus ivory that had been given up years before by the other Eskimos of western Alaska. They still adhered strictly to the elaborate ceremonies relating to seal hunting as well as their religious and social life in general. Seal and fish are plentiful around the island and form the staple of their diet.

Under the Department of Agriculture the island has been made a bird and game reservation. In 1935 and 1936 thirty-one musk oxen were imported from Greenland and transferred to the island. Domestication experiments have been in progress and the herd, slowly increasing, now numbers more than a hundred. Musk oxen formerly roamed throughout most of the Polar Regions. Generally speaking, this animal and man do not occupy the same country for they do not flee and so are exterminated by arrow and spear. The last Alaskan musk ox was killed south of Point Barrow about 1867 or 1870.

Marvelously adapted to their environment, musk oxen have a perfect defense against all northern predatory animals except the grizzly bear, which has been successful in killing them around Fairbanks during domestication experiments there. Wolves, which are absent from Nunivak, they do not fear, nor do wolves attack them unless they come upon a lone animal, which is rare.

Musk oxen seldom attack. When alarmed they run to the top of the nearest knoll and make a defensive formation, with the big animals outside and the calves in the center. They charge singly usually, each one making a short rush of from ten to fifteen yards, then whirling, running back to the herd, facing about and backing into line.

The entire body of this tough northern animal is covered with long, straggling, stiff black hair, similar in quality to a horse's mane. In the roots of this hair grows a soft wool which is shed every spring, in April or May, while the long, stiff hair remains permanently. They are short legged, and during the

106

Musk Oxen

shedding season you cannot see their legs at all from a side view, so long is the wool. This shedding wool drags in long tags after the animal and wisps of it may be picked up from the ground.

The meat of the musk oxen is practically indistinguishable from domestic beef in flavor or odor, and the milk they give is rich and creamy. Their wool, soft and fine as cashmere, will not shrink, as most wool does, even when washed in hot water and rubbed. What a perfect domestic animal they will make! They are better than cattle because they supply wool in addition to meat; they are better than sheep for supplying wool, because they are three times as large; they are easy to look after for they are naturally disinclined to roam and can defend themselves against wolves.

As implied by its name, musk ox meat was supposed to smell strongly of musk; but all the explorers who have lived on it deny this. In fact Sverdrup, the Norwegian explorer, unable to detect any odor of musk, renamed them "polar oxen" which seems more suitable. The Latin name for the animal is *ovibos* which means "sheep cow," and "polar cattle" has also been suggested.

In addition to domesticating polar oxen, reindeer breeding experiments are also being conducted on the island.

White foxes regularly migrate to Nunivak for the winter and return to the mainland in the spring, using the ice floes as a ferry.

Cape Etolin, named after the explorer who was governor of the Russian America Company from 1841 to 1845, is one of the two small sections of the island adequately charted. It is a narrow peninsula, part of which becomes an island at high tide; to the east of it lies the native village.

The Russian America Company of which Etolin was governor was an organization similar to Canada's Hudson's Bay Company which had exclusive trading rights in Alaska before it was purchased by the United States.

ST. LAWRENCE ISLAND AND REINDEER

As we continue our journey northward, the next island in our path is St. Lawrence, the largest in Bering Sea and about one hundred and ten miles southwest of King Island. Another stepping stone from the Old World to the New, this volcanic island was undoubtedly part of the land bridge that once connected the two continents.

While Bering is the accredited discoverer of St. Lawrence Island, it is probable that earlier Russian traders and explorers saw it first. Bering in his diary for August 10, 1728 writes: "We located this island which we named St. Lawrence, in honor of the day." The first settlers of St. Lawrence Island were, no doubt, a part of that ancient migration of Asiatics who by two streams, one through the Diomedes and the other through the Aleutians, became the ancestors of the peoples of North and South America.

The island is only forty miles away from Siberia, a distance easily covered by umiak, but it is one hundred and eighteen miles from the nearest Alaska mainland. Because it is much nearer to Siberia, it is natural that the natives have been in intimate contact with their Siberian cousins. Its remoteness from Alaska has served to guard its Eskimos from the "civilizing" influence of the white man and, until fairly recently, they retained almost intact their Eskimo way of life. They are still a meat-eating people. There has been considerable change in their style of clothing, which has been due mainly to the introduction of inexpensive cotton material out of which the women make

The sidewalks of St. Lawrence Island

dresses patterned after ours, to be worn indoors. Eskimos formerly stripped to the waist indoors, women and men alike, and kept their houses heated to what we would think of as uncomfortably hot temperatures. When the missionaries informed the women that it was immodest to sit around half naked, the Eskimo women, whose ideas of modesty differ greatly from ours, thought it strange; but eager to please, they began wearing their cotton housedresses indoors and it is now an established custom. By now, too, they understand our ideas of modesty as one more "taboo" which they are careful to observe.

A taboo is an act that is forbidden through religious or superstitious belief. For instance, among certain Eskimos it is taboo to carve or chop wood the day after killing a polar bear. In another section certain parts of meat are taboo or forbidden to women. Eskimos are not the only people who have taboos, although primitive peoples as a rule have a greater number than civilized folk. To some civilized people it is taboo to walk under a ladder and among theatrical folk it is taboo to whistle in an actor's dressing room.

To get back to St. Lawrence Island, from which we seem to have drifted, the island, about a hundred miles long and twenty miles wide, is a government reservation. That is, the government has set aside the island for the exclusive use of the Eskimo inhabitants, like the great Indian reservations of western United States.

In 1900 the Department of the Interior placed seventy imported Siberian reindeer on the island to provide food and clothing for the natives. Today there are ten thousand animals, all descendants of the original seventy. They provide hides and fawnskins for bedding and clothing and delicious meat for food. Reindeer, by the way, is the same animal as caribou, except that reindeer is domesticated and caribou is wild. If associated with enough to keep them tame and protected from their chief enemy, the wolf, reindeer will double their numbers every three years, which accounts for the enormous increase of the animals on St. Lawrence. And while increasing they have each year provided food, clothing and bedding besides being a fine insurance against famine in case their other hunting and fishing should fail.

The Eskimos of St. Lawrence Island, numbering about five hundred, are among the most prosperous in Alaska. Among the rolling grassy hills are many fresh-water streams and innumerable lakes. The long coast line, in the direct path of the ice pack, is well located for securing food and fur. The ice brings

110

Reindeer is the domesticated caribou

with it those animals that live on or by the ice, walrus, seal, white fox and whale. In summer countless numbers of migrating birds also make St. Lawrence Island their home.

Foxes, numerous on the island, in addition to those which come ashore from the ice pack, and the ivory carvings made by the natives provide the chief sources of cash income. So prosperous are some of the people that families have two sewing machines, two alarm clocks, and two or more of many other expensive imported items.

Sevuokuk, which Alaskans call Gambell, and Savoonga are the two settlements on the island. Each has a mayor and council elected by popular vote to administer the affairs of the group. Teachers and a nurse from the Bureau of Indian Affairs, with an occasional missionary, look after the general welfare of the inhabitants. Each village has a cooperative store, which is designed to enable its members to sell its wares at a greater profit by dealing directly with the purchaser, eliminating the middleman, or wholesaler. The cooperatives are managed by a native board of directors which elects the storekeepers and the chief reindeer herders, sets prices and takes care of families when the trapping is poor. The sales of the beautiful fox pelts and ivory carvings are usually handled through these stores.

The mothers on St. Lawrence Island have a unique method of carrying their children. Most, in fact all, Alaskan Eskimo mothers carry their babies from birth until they are able to walk, on the backs, inside their coats. As soon as the St. Lawrence Island children are able to sit up, they perch on their mothers' shoulders twining their feet around her neck. A mother will often grip a child's arm and foot in each of her hands to keep him steady if she is moving quickly, but on the whole the child develops a fine sense of balance and can usually manage to keep upright.

The St. Matthew Islands, including St. Matthew, Hall and Pinnacle Islands, are rocky and uninhabited; they lie about one hundred and thirty-five miles westward of Nunivak. It is said that a few Russians were left on the islands the winter of 1816 to collect sealskins and that all of them died of starvation. This must have been through mismanagement, for whalers have reported that St. Matthew is a rendezvous for many white bears and call it Bear Island. It is the southern limit for the large floating fields of ice which bring with them an abundance of game — the so-called pack ice. Precipitous, foggy and poorly charted, these islands are seldom visited.

Two baby polar bears

About sixty miles southeast of the Diomedes, is an island of solid granite about two miles square that rises steeply from the sea. Discovered by Captain Cook in 1778, King Island is inhabited by a community of about one hundred and eighty cliff-dwellers, for there is no flat land on the island. The Eskimos have built their village on the sheltered side of the steep island. The backs of their wooden cliff dwellings rest on the rocky precipice; the fronts are supported by slender wooden poles which may be as much as forty feet above the cliff. The houses are covered and lashed securely with green walrus hides which dry hard and tight, forming a tough weatherproof covering.

The living quarters of each house average about eight square feet with ceilings so low that one cannot stand upright. On the floor of these little houses the people sit, eat and sleep, while outside the house proper is a long shed in which all household and hunting gear not in use is stored.

Long community houses, called Karrigi or Kajigi, where the young unmarried men of the crowded village sleep, are also the community workshops. There are three of these on King Island. The male population of the island keeps its tool chests at the Kajigi and it is here that sleds are built, hunting gear fashioned and repaired, a new covering put on an umiak, or skin boat, in fact any work that requires tools and a large working space. The Kajigi is also the gathering place for songs, dancing and story-telling; all highly developed arts among the Eskimos.

It has been said, with a good deal of truth, that the climate of King Island is divided into two seasons — four months of fog and eight months of ice. When you look at the view of King Island from the sea on page 115, you might think the film had been spoiled by being carelessly exposed to the light, but this is an actual picture of the way the island looks most of the time during the foggy season.

The waters surrounding King Island are rich in seals and other marine life and the King Islanders, famous as hunters, are seldom troubled for want of food. Migratory birds leave millions of eggs each year and in the spring huge walrus herds follow the breakup of the ice and come by the thousands from their native Siberia. Warned by lookouts atop the island, who spot the herd, the Eskimos, clad in white for camouflage, push out to sea in their umiaks.

The cliff dwellers of King Island have built their villages on the side of an island of solid rock. The two largest buildings in the foggy settlement are the schoolhouse and the church

Dogs snooze comfortably and Eskimos live happily forty feet above ground

Grounding their boats on the nearest ice cake, at a pre-arranged signal, they shoot. The season is short and the hunters work night and day while it lasts. When the animals are cut up, what meat cannot be used immediately is frozen and placed in a natural cold-storage plant in a cleft in the side of the island, where it remains fresh for years, very much like the quick frozen foods offered by our corner grocery.

There are large rectangles scattered throughout the village on King Island. These are tightly stretched walrus skins drying on their driftwood frames. Walrus hides are so thick they cannot be used for skin boat coverings unless they are split. The Eskimos have invented a way of splitting the skin exactly in half, making two skins from one. This is usually done by a woman

116

*The streets of the King Island village are long high rows of wooden steps that
climb upward higher and higher*

with her moon-shaped ulu, or woman's knife. With a rocking motion, holding
one hand beneath to feel the thickness, the skin is split into two even pieces
without making a hole in either one.

The roofs of their houses are made of the younger male walrus skins
which also provide coverings for their umiaks. The meat, of course, is eaten
and considered especially good. A salable part is the ivory tusks from which
the skillful King Islanders carve beautiful trinkets. These they sell to tourists
in Nome during their annual summer visit.

Each summer the whole population leaves the island for Nome. They
make the trip in their skin boats, most of which are now equipped with the
latest model outboard motors. In Nome they live in rude huts or under the

117

This enormous old walrus has been killed, hauled up on the ice, and is now ready to be cut up

Landing an umiak or skin boat on rocky King Island

tipped-up skin boats, selling their ivory salt shakers, ash trays, egg cups and cribbage boards to the tourists. They carve these from white, pearly, fresh ivory tusks and from "fossil" ivory obtained from ancient mammoth tusks. Carved tools and weapons, made for their own consumption, are illustrated with events of daily life carved in delicate line etchings or in low relief.

The crossing from King Island to the mainland is usually made in July, and the islanders stay for about two months, or until they have sold their wares and visited all their friends. In the fall, when the weather is uncertain and the crossing dangerous, they return to their island with dogs, umiaks, and supplies aboard the U. S. Coast Guard cutter, in fine Navy style.

Sailing about sixty-five miles to the northwest brings us back again to the Diomedes, where little Diomede stands looking into tomorrow.

WHY HAS Alaska suddenly assumed such tremendous importance in the war? Before 1940 Alaska was the "forgotten land." Little was known about her and much of that little was incorrect. Today most people know that Alaska matters. What Seward had said from a naval point of view was stated from an aeronautical viewpoint by the late General Billy Mitchell, who said: "Alaska is the most central place in the world for aircraft, and that is true either of Europe, Asia or North America, for whoever holds Alaska will hold the world, and I think it is the most important place in the world."

There were many who laughed loud and long at General Mitchell's statement when it was made, but more recently the laughs have been fewer and farther between. He has been proven right about so many other things that his writings are now being dug out and quoted respectfully.

121

In 1940 the first detachment of troops arrived in Alaska to start work on the air base at Anchorage. At first a mere handful of men, they lived in snow covered tents until barracks could be built to house them. Work was begun at a feverish rate. Boats that once had brought tourists, now brought defense workers, soldiers, construction material and supplies. Anchorage became alive with busy workers. Soldiers were soon arriving faster than the barracks could be built.

With Alaska's small population, most of the labor for the vast construction program had to be imported. The lack of any overland connection with the States was a handicap, and undeveloped resources made necessary the shipment of supplies of food as well as materials for the workers and soldiers. Seven days a week they worked in summer, in daylight and darkness, and the work is still going on. From a comparative wilderness grew, in an incredibly short time, comfortable barracks and huge plane hangars. Nearby Elmendorf Field's concrete runways were finished and soon roaring with the comforting noise of bombers and fighter planes. Anchorage became headquarters for the Alaska Defense Command. A small miracle had been accomplished!

Founded in 1914 as a construction camp for the Alaska Railroad, Anchorage was government managed until 1920 when the Federal Government relinquished its control of town affairs. Elections were held, a council chosen and the decision was made to incorporate as a town. Good motor roads branch out from Anchorage connecting it with nearby mines and farms. The general offices and repair shops of the Alaska Railroad are located here and the Anchorage *Times,* a daily newspaper is published. No mining is done in the immediate vicinity, but Anchorage is a center for outlying quartz and placer gold mining and coal mining. Fishing, canning and some fur farming and trapping are the other industries.

Once again, in 1942, Anchorage is virtually a government town, for the Army has created a boom through the building of Fort Richardson in the vicinity. The population was 3,488 in 1940 but by 1941 there were already as many soldiers at the Fort as people in the town.

When the news of Pearl Harbor reached Alaska, a feeling of tenseness gripped most Alaskans, for they knew how vulnerable is her position and the threat of possible bombings was very real. But Alaska got busy. By nightfall a total blackout was in effect, and still is, at coastal towns anywhere near Army

122

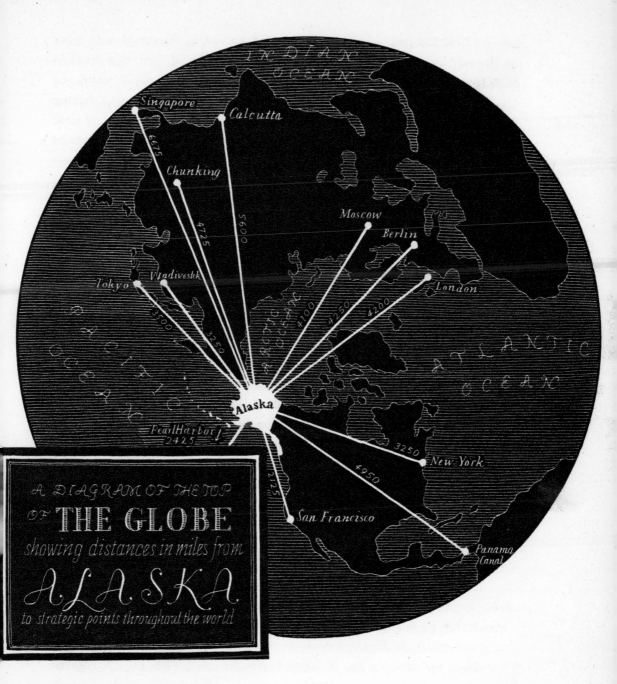

Singapore · 6475

Calcutta

Chunking · 4725

5600

Moscow

Berlin

Vladivostok

Tokyo · 3100 · 3250

London

4100 · 4250 · 4200

PACIFIC OCEAN

ATLANTIC OCEAN

Alaska

PearlHarbor · 2425

3250 · New York

2125

4950

San Francisco

Panama Canal

INDIAN OCEAN

ARCTIC OCEAN

A DIAGRAM OF THE TOP
OF **THE GLOBE**
showing distances in miles from
ALASKA
to strategic points throughout the world

bases. Plans were made and carried out for the evacuation of the wives and children of Army personnel and construction workers to the States. Home Guards were formed in almost every town. Even the old sourdoughs, those old timers who came north for the Gold Rush and who acquired their name from the sour dough biscuits they made, were organized for guerilla warfare.

Alaska was awake!

The Eskimos too, are taking part. Many of the men have enlisted in the Army and the women at Nome are hard at work making their beautiful light-weight coldproof caribou suits for Army troops at cold weather stations.

Boys from the southern states are learning to ski and "mush," which is the Alaskan term for running behind a sled and driving a team of dogs. They are learning to take care of themselves in all kinds of weather and to fight in Arctic and sub-Arctic country. Many of them have fallen in love with the country and plan, when the war is over, to settle there permanently.

THE CAPITAL—OLD AND NEW

When we purchased Alaska in 1867 the Russian capital of Alaska was at Sitka. Today Sitka is probably the most Russian of all Alaskan cities and almost everywhere you look are reminders that this was once a thriving Russian city with an observatory, a museum, a hospital with forty beds, and several schools where boys learned the rudiments of mechanics, navigation and accounting. The city was founded in 1799 when a Siberian trader, Alexander Baranof came from Kodiak Isand with thirty Russians and several hundred Aleuts to Sitka. He was armed with a charter from the Russian America Company, which had exclusive rights to all profits to be derived from every form of resource in Russian America; he was under orders to stop the trade in furs and ivory being carried on by other nations. He was also to protect the Indians in their life and property, to feed them in time of disaster, to educate their children and, if possible, to save their souls.

The Indians, unaware of this intended kindness, resisted the newcomers vigorously. Ten of the thirty Russians had constantly to stand on guard; the local people would capture and murder any single man or small group of Russians. In 1802 when Baranof was visiting Kodiak Island, they captured the post, killing all the men and taking the women and children prisoners.

Trapper in Sitka, with his winter's catch

Baranof returned in 1804 and rebuilt the village, naming it New Archangel. The Tlingit Indian word, Sitka, which means the "best place," had long been in use, however, and the new name did not stick. The hostility between the Indians and the whites continued until as late as 1855 when a battle cost the lives of twenty Russians and sixty Indians.

As the capital of Russian America, Sitka was, at the end of the eighteenth century, the center of trade and civilization for the whole northwest coast. In her harbor were clipper ships from New England, which stopped on their way to China; English traders, ships from far off Kronstadt on the Baltic, Spanish ships, French ships! Here Yankee traders matched wits with Tlingit Indians, the Yankees frequently getting the worst of it, their reputation for wooden nutmegs to the contrary notwithstanding. It was the gayest and most brilliant city on the Pacific coast.

Costly ornaments, works of art and fine furniture were all imported from Russia to furnish in grand style Baranof's rough-hewn castle fortress. Great families at St. Petersburg even contributed 1200 volumes for the library. Baranof, a harsh administrator, was feared but respected. He retired at the age of seventy-two and was on the way home when he died and was buried at sea.

Sitka, as the Russian capital was the scene of the dramatic formal transfer of the Territory of Alaska from Russia to the United States. It was on October 18, 1867 with Russian soldiers in their dark red-trimmed uniforms, and United States troops in full dress uniform that the Commissioner of the Imperial Ruler of all the Russians said the few necessary words to the Commissioner for the United States who received the Territory. Lined up in front of the Governor's castle, they made a brave show despite the rain. The Russian flag was lowered and the American flag raised in its place to the accompaniment of salutes from the batteries and of the guns from the ships in the harbor. Most of the Russians went back to their native land as soon as they were able but some remained in the new land and their descendants still live at Sitka.

Today Sitka is a modern town of over two thousand. You approach it by steamer going through a beautiful narrow channel that runs between it and Japonski Island where the Navy maintains a station. It is here that you get your first view of Mount Edgecombe, which frames the town considered one of the most picturesque in Alaska. The innumerable little islands that surround

126

Bishop of Greek Catholic Church in Sitka

Sitka offer many long, calm lagoons which make perfect landing places for planes equipped with pontoons. This was an important factor in the Navy's selection of Sitka for one of its three Naval bases in Alaska. There are hotels and radio stations, library and cold storage plant. One of the most fascinating sights to be seen here is the Sitka National Monument Park which contains one of the largest collection of totem poles, eighteen in number, from all parts of Alaska. At the grand Cathedral of St. Michael services are still conducted in Russian for all still holding to the old Russian Orthodox religion.

Sitka remained the capital of Alaska until 1900 when the rapidly growing city of Juneau was named the new capital. Governor Brady and the executive offices, however, remained in Sitka until 1906 when Brady was removed from office; the new governor took up his duties at Juneau.

Juneau, still the capital, stands on Gastineau Channel at the water's edge, framed by the steep, timbered slopes of Mt. Juneau and Mt. Roberts which tower above the city. In fact so little space is left at the base of these mountains one wonders how a town came to be built here. The answer is easy — gold. Juneau's history, like many an Alaskan town begins with the story of that yellow metal. Two prospectors, Harris and Juneau, found gold at Silver Bow Basin in 1880, and before the next spring more than a hundred men had camped at the site. This was the first gold rush on Alaskan soil. Harris and Juneau disagreed for two years about the naming of their camp and finally a town meeting of miners was held which arrived at a compromise by calling the town Juneau and the district Harrisburg. Although Juneau was officially made the capital of Alaska in 1900, the executive offices were not moved from Sitka until 1906. The beautiful Federal building, finished in 1931 at a cost of $1,0000,000, houses the Territorial Legislature and the U. S. District Court, as well as many other Federal and Territorial Departments.

Gold mining is the chief industry of Juneau. The Alaska Juneau Mine, from the standpoint of tons mined, is the largest gold operation in the world. The mine employs nine hundred men and has an annual payroll of over $1,500,000. Salmon and halibut fishing come next in importance, and there is a good deal of fur farming. There is some agriculture, but scarcely enough to supply local needs. There is too much rain for growing grains, but vegetables and small fruits do well.

Juneau has a fine harbor that offers excellent docking facilities for large and small boats. It is the headquarters port for the Customs District of Alaska and over 500 steam and motor vessels make it their home port. Launches maintain weekly schedules between the town and small communities near by and a bridge spans the channel to Douglas Island, a mountainous, wooded mass with barren peaks rising above the timber line.

The most modern town in Alaska, Juneau has tall buildings, two movie theatres, public libraries and two daily newspapers.

Nearby is the magnificent Mendenhall Glacier, one of the few glaciers in the world accessible by automobile road. Seventeen miles long, the ice stream in places is a beautiful blue where crevasses reflect the color of the water. It is a favorite haunt of tourists.

Juneau, the capital of Alaska

The word *gold* has a glamorous sound! Its magic was the lure that brought thousands of hopefuls to Alaska at the beginning of the century. Some believed there were fortunes to be made overnight; some were sick of cities and wanted to draw breaths of clear air in unexplored places. For many of the older men it was the last hope of a quick success. A few women, considered very daring, came too. Idealists and cynics; workers and loafers; explorers and adventurers; they all came. There was plenty of room for them in Alaska.

Some struck gold but more of them, after varying degrees of perseverance, gave up prospecting and turned to keeping shops, restaurants and roadhouses. Those who knew a trade like carpentering found it more lucrative than gold hunting. These "sourdoughs" formed the backbone of many an Alaskan town.

In 1902 Felix Pedro discovered gold on what is now Pedro Creek. In September of the same year a group of the first stampeders held a meeting, appointed a recorder and named the place Fairbanks, after the vice-president.

While news of the strike spread rapidly, there was disappointment in many a heart when it was found that the gold bearing bedrock was buried eighty to 100 feet under muck and gravel. This meant that expensive equipment was needed on a large scale in order to extract the gold. While it was hard on the lone prospector, it prevented the kind of mushroom development that almost wrecked Nome and Dawson, in Canada. Fairbanks has its gaudy memories, all right, but nothing like the wild, extravagant disorder which was typical of Nome, prevailed. Instead of the colorful adventurous prospector, there are now high salaried business executives; instead of rocky, swampy roads there are automobiles, trains and even airplanes. For in many sections around Fairbanks the rich pay dirt was worked out years ago and it is only through mass production that mining there now can be made to pay. The machinery is costly and only large corporations are able to operate.

Gold mining is still the principal industry of Fairbanks but logging and lumbering are gaining in importance. The use of the airplane has become an important factor in gold mining operations in the vicinity. The prospector or miner today can step into an airplane and be landed with his equipment in a few hours during any season at a camp which formerly could be reached only in

Fairbanks at noon in the middle of winter

winter and by dog team. Additional supplies can also be flown in at arranged intervals.

Fairbanks, a bustling metropolis in the valley of the Tanana River (a branch of the Yukon), 120 miles south of the Arctic Circle, is called the "golden heart" of Alaska. Geographically it is almost the center of Alaska and the golden thread that runs throughout so much of Alaska's history played a part in its founding. This greatly expanded mining camp is the northern terminus of the Government-owned and operated Alaska Railroad. Its modest homes of one story peeled log cabins are heated with wood-burning stoves and surrounded by flower gardens. The more pretentious dwellings are of frame construction with cement foundations, bathrooms and furnaces and are bordered by cement sidewalks on the main street and planks on the outskirts of the town.

Fairbanks has a financial and commercial importance far beyond the actual size of its population, which was 3304 in 1940. It has far more conveniences for a town of its size than a city in the States, they include telephone, telegraph,

131

electricity, radio station, hospital, Chamber of Commerce, churches and several labor unions.

During the long summer days, which darken only to a bright twilight around midnight, the temperatures frequently rise to 90° in the shade, with a maximum of 99°. About one hundred miles south of the Arctic circle, Fairbanks does not have quite the extremes of heat recorded at Fort Yukon, a hundred miles farther north, but still the vicinity is perhaps the best farming region of Alaska, especially for cereals. It is said to be easier to raise tomatoes in the Tanana Valley than in the Matanuska Valley five hundred miles farther south. Wheat is a much safer crop than at Matanuska and the quality is better. Indeed the grain is seldom injured by frost except in valley bottoms.

Still there has been little agricultural development near Fairbanks in proportion to the suitability of soil and climate. People are busy gold mining, wages are high, and in any case there is the custom of importing things from outside. The Alaskan of the Fairbanks vicinity is not the farming pioneer we think of as working frugally on his own land, producing most of what he eats and wears. On the contrary, it is the Fairbanks practice to sell most of what you produce and buy most of what you use, which is the modern commercial outlook and not the old style farm pioneering of the Abraham Lincoln type.

The frostless season of midsummer, though long enough for the ripening of wheat, is but a small part of the working year with reference to the gold mining. Even the dredges, which operate with liquid water, keep running for a number of weeks after the freeze-up in the fall and start again in the spring long before such spring thaws as are useful to farmers. The quartz mining runs through the twelve months of the year. Typical wages in the summertime have been $6 to $8 for boys of high school age, with board and room. Competent "unskilled" miners have been getting $10 and $12 a day; those in the quartz mines drawing that pay for the year around, with meals and lodging.

With winter, the nights grow longer. The cold grows more intense. Some winters the thermometer drops to 60° and 70° below; but then the air becomes breathlessly still, for you never have a wind at extremely low temperatures. Some activity is curtailed, but mail, freight, and passengers still come in over the Alaska Railroad, planes arrive daily, and the North Pole bakery freezes thousands of loaves of bread that will be as fresh as when baked six weeks later when they are thawed out in the ovens of outlying camps.

The building of the government railroad meant as much to Fairbanks as the Union Pacific meant to the Pacific Coast, giving it a tremendous spurt of new life. Freight and supplies arriving by railroad or highway are transported still farther into the interior by the Fairbanks fleet of twelve hundred autos and trucks over a highway system totaling twelve hundred miles, or directly through the air by plane. In summer steamboats ply the Tanana from nearby Nenana to the Yukon.

The gold rush at Fairbanks was a Sunday school picnic in a New England town compared to the Nome gold rush. Almost all the wild and extravagant tales told about the good old gold rush days probably happened at Nome.

It was in September, 1896 that John Brynteson, Erick O. Lundblum and Jafet Lindeberg discovered rich "pay dirt" on Anvil Creek, and as soon as the news leaked out of Nome, the gold rush was on. By the next summer tents were pitched on the beach at the mouth of the Snake River where the town of Nome now stands. When the news reached Seattle, the transportation companies, which were getting high prices for passengers and freight, exaggerated the prospects considerably, until people were wild to get to Nome where they were told one could get fabulously rich almost overnight.

The site of Nome has no harbor of any kind. Ship after ship dumped passengers and freight on the beach in utter confusion, with no shelter or protection of any kind. Streets were laid out parallel to the waterfront but rain soon transformed them into a thick mire.

Along with the highest type of pioneer and prospector came the lowest; saloons, gambling houses and dives mushroomed. Drunkenness and gambling were commonplace and scarcely a day went by without a murder.

Then gold was discovered in the very sands of the beach of Nome. The General Land Office ruled that claims could not be staked on land below high tide and the right to pan gold on the beach was as free as the right to fish. There was no hazardous journey over mountains and glaciers, as in the Klondike; you could come by steamer all the way and then you simply washed the gold up out of the sand. Excitement was intense. Fortunes were made and spent overnight. People arrived from the States at the rate of a thousand a day; soon there was not even tent room. Ten thousand would-be prospectors, many of whom had spent their last cent for passage, were stranded on the beach. It was not long before the drinking water was contaminated, and small-pox, typhoid and pneumonia followed.

Many of the stranded gold-seekers were taken back to the States in revenue

133

cutters, but others stayed to hunt for gold in other districts and to work on the railroads being built.

The tales of fortunes made overnight were pleasantly remembered; the tales of death, disease and failure quickly forgotten. The community of Nome prospered and grew; many more gold fields were discovered and worked. Today with a population of about a thousand, two-thirds of whom are white, the town has changed considerably and the most exciting event of the year is the famous All-Alaska Championship Dog Race from Nome to Golovin and return.

In 1934 a disastrous fire swept Nome, destroying most of the business section. In reconstruction, the advantage was taken to erect modern, permanent buildings, straighten sidewalks and widen streets. Today Nome is no longer a city of dance halls, saloons and stampeders but the central trading post of a large still-to-be-developed area.

The origin of the name of Nome has been disputed. Many think that it is the result of a draftsman's error. According to this view a chart was being drawn of the coast; a certain point was nameless and the draftsman wrote "?Name" opposite to it. When the chart was hurriedly inked in, *?Name* was read by the cartographer as C. Nome! Cape Nome it has been ever since, and the town was named after the cape.

THE FARTHEST NORTH COLLEGE

Only four miles from Fairbanks is the farthest-north college in North America, the University of Alaska. On the side of a hill lie its eight small buildings surrounded by one of the most magnificent views in Alaska. The distant Alaska Range forms a cyclorama behind the buildings and on clear days students can see Mount McKinley from their classroom windows.

Starting with only six students in 1922, the University had nearly three hundred by 1941 and its credits are accepted everywhere. As the president of the college has often said: "Nobody is *sent* to college here." Boys rustle freight and dig ditches and the girls find some sort of employment in and around town to pay their expenses. It is believed that a larger percentage of students work their way through the University of Alaska than any other college in the country. There is no tuition fee for Alaskans, and board and room can be

Gold mining is the second industry of Alaska

obtained cheaply. Alaskans make up two thirds, or three quarters, of the students, the rest usually migrate from the states for the opportunity of working their way through college. The students do most of the work on the campus, some of them waiting on tables to defray expenses. Much of the food is supplied by the college's own Agricultural Experiment Station which is near the campus and where students have a chance to work out in practice what they learn in theory. While the college offers both natives and whites the traditional liberal arts courses, most of the emphasis is on mining and metallurgy, agriculture, engineering and geology. Courses are offered in chemistry, home economics, business administration and arts and letters. Many adults in Fairbanks enroll at the University during the enforced winter idleness.

The School of Mines is perfectly located; for within a radius of twenty miles of the campus are found almost every possible kind of mining, including lode mines, gold dredges, hydraulic, shovel dragline and drift placer mines. As soon as students learn the first principles of mining, field trips are arranged and theories are demonstrated. Classroom and field work is arranged so that young engineers leave the University with first hand knowledge of every phase of mining operations as well as every type of mining.

On the slope of the campus hill is housed a complete mill for refining gold ores. Here again the students are trained to take part in the actual operation, and ores submitted by miners throughout the territory are tested. For the school of mines is the highest authority in Alaska on mining problems and is frequently consulted.

During the summer the students get no vacations. Summer is the time when most of them earn enough money to keep them going another year at school. Some take part in the seasonal activities centered around Fairbanks, but many go to distant mining camps to try out their new-learned skills. Some work in the nearby gold mines not only earning money but gaining valuable experience.

While most of the students are hard working, serious minded youngsters, they miss none of the fun that most colleges offer in the way of organized sports. Hockey and baseball are played in spring and fall, and skiing is the most popular sport for both boys and girls in winter. Their Fight Song goes: "Cheer for the Polar Bears, Mighty Men Are They." *The Farthest North Collegian,* the school paper, is an eight page, six column affair, published on the

Gold mining dredge at Fairbanks

first of every month and contains general campus news and interesting educational articles.

Through the courtesy of Fairbanks Radio Station KFAR the University sponsors two fifteen minute programs a week, giving students practical and valuable radio experience.

The University also has a fine museum started as a result of Otto W. Geist's expeditions to St. Lawrence Island. More than 75,000 specimens make up the Geist collection and historical items relating to early Alaskan history are also being collected.

Strangely enough, one of the richest sources of fossil skeletal remains of prehistoric animals has been the gold mining companies! From the dredging operations of the companies on nearby creeks in and around Fairbanks large quantities of the bones of prehistoric animals that once roamed Alaska have been rescued. The American Museum of Natural History in New York cooperating with the University of Alaska and the U. S. Smelting Refining and Mining Company has retained part of the collection another part remaining at the University museum. In some cases where the ground has been permanently frozen for hundreds of centuries, animals with the flesh still attached to their bones have been excavated, perfectly preserved by their icy graves.

Another field where students may gain practical as well as theoretical experience at the University of Alaska is in the field of Anthropology. Each summer field trips under the sponsorship of the University, and sometimes in charge of one of the professors are made to study both the Indians and the Eskimos. In connection with this study much archeological work is accomplished. One of the most startling and important finds of the century was made in 1939 and 1940 by Professor of Anthropology Froelich G. Rainey and his colleagues. Under the sponsorship of the University and the American Museum of Natural History in New York, the party found at Point Hope, on Bering Sea, an ancient city of about eight hundred houses arranged in streets, which must have had a population larger than the modern city of Fairbanks! All this was discovered north of 68°, about 130 miles beyond the Arctic Circle.

Ipiutak, as the location of this ancient city is called by the present Eskimos, must have been built before the Christian era; two thousand years is thought a conservative estimate of its age. The excavations have yielded beautiful ivory carvings unlike any known Eskimo or other American Indian culture of the

Since Nome has no harbor even passengers must be lightered aboard ship by barges. Here is the last barge load about to be taken out to the last ship leaving Nome for Seattle before the freezeup

northern regions. Fashioned of logs, the strange tombs gave up skeletons which stared up at the excavators with artificial eyeballs carved of ivory and inlaid with jet. Apparently, before burial, the natural eyes had been gouged out and replaced with ivory ones. Mouth covers, and nose plugs of ivory carved to represent birds, added to the fantastic appearance of the skeletons which had been buried with exquisite carvings of walrus ivory with spiral decorations. Numerous delicately made and engraved implements, also found in the graves, resembled some of those produced in North China two or three thousand years ago; others resemble carvings of the Ainu peoples in northern Japan and the natives of the Amur River in Siberia.

The material culture of these people was not a simple one, of the kind usually found in the Arctic, but elaborate and that of a sophisticated people, in this sense more advanced than any known Eskimos, and clearly derived from eastern Asia, whence these people doubtless emigrated.

The life of the present inhabitants of Point Hope, or Tigara, The Fore Finger, as the Eskimos call it, centers around the pursuit of the large bowhead whale.

In April, May and early June of each year the whales migrate northward along the open shore lead, heading for Point Barrow and the Arctic Ocean. A lead (pronounced leed) is a strip of open water between fields of ice which may be yards or miles wide and which is opened by the combined forces of current and wind; the shore lead is the water lane between the stationary land-fast ice and the moving pack farther out.

Weeks of preparation precede the coming of the whales; all gear used in whaling must be clean and, if possible, new. According to belief, the whale cannot see the new gear, but if he does he is pleased, for it means that knives are sharp and will not hurt in the butchering. Skin boats are repaired, spruce-wood paddles are scraped clean, harpoon shafts, boat hooks and lances made ready. Throughout the bustle of preparation the women nowadays provide bowls of *makpaurat,* a modern dish of white flour doughnuts or crullers, fried in seal oil. These are a special feast to the crowds of children.

Soon after the feast the hunters take off by dog team, the hunters themselves helping to pull the boats and gear across the ice until the lead of open water is reached. They camp at the edge of the lead and stay as long as the lead remains open, getting meanwhile as many whales as possible. Sometimes

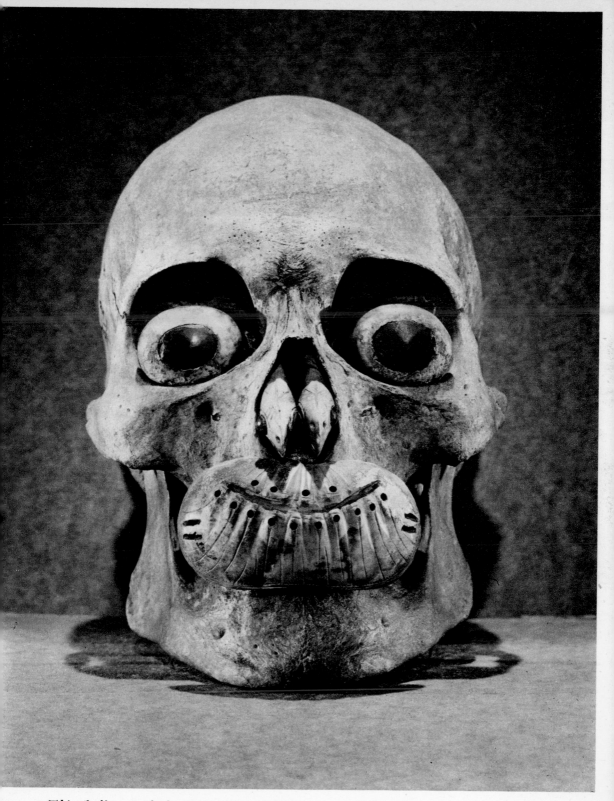

This skull unearthed at Point Hope has ivory eyes inlaid with pupils of jet, and ivory nose plug and mouth cover

the ice will begin to break up without warning; gear may be lost and hunters separated. This is only one of the many dangers that await those who would secure the mighty bowhead, next to the blue whale of the Antarctic, largest creature in the world. However, this type of whaling is not more dangerous than many of our regular occupations, such as taxi driving or coal mining.

Every part of the whale is utilized. Drumheads are made from the skin of the liver and lungs, net sinkers from the ribs, woven baskets from the baleen. The jawbones are set up as monuments or used in buildings, for instance as door frames for houses or outer porches.

The day after the boats have returned to shore comes a great feast, often lasting three days. It is climaxed by *Nalukataktut*, a ceremony or game from which the feast derives its name. Forty or fifty people grasp a large walrus hide and toss a performer fifteen or twenty feet high in the air. The object is to remain upright, to land on one's feet each time, which only the expert can do; the novice falls on his back and is at the mercy of the blanket tossers. The tossing is accompanied by singing and drums. This sport, which combines a kind of terror with joyous excitement, was perhaps formerly performed only at the time of the whaling feast, which was the high spot of the year. Now it is part of any hilarious celebration, particularly the Fourth of July and especially at places like Nome.

The University maintains one of several agricultural experiment stations near Matanuska. Six miles northeast of Matanuska on a branch of the Alaska Railroad is the "Matanuska Colony" at the town of Palmer. This is the working center of the Alaska Rural Rehabilitation Corporation which transported about one hundred and seventy families from the drought-stricken areas of the middle-western states, and from other localities, to Alaska to start life anew. It was in May, 1935, that colonists chosen from the relief rolls of northern Minnesota, Wisconsin and Michigan arrived at Palmer. At first they lived in tents until the land was cleared and houses and barns were built. Money for equipment, purchase of land, buildings, livestock and furniture was lent by the Federal Government. By the fall of 1936, the farmers' newly built barns were bulging with harvested crops, and Palmer had grown into a flourishing town.

As usual in a large project, there were some discontented ones who deserted the colony. Their stories were picked up by the newspapers and broadcast to the nation, giving the impression that the experiment was a failure. There

Whalers carrying their umiak to the open lead. Goggles are worn to prevent snow blindness

Harpooning a bowhead whale off Point Hope, where it is still hunted for food

Dissecting a newly caught white whale. Pieces of the skin with the blubber attached are eaten both raw and cooked by the Eskimos, who consider it a great delicacy

were mistakes, yes, but failure — no. The land of the dissatisfied colonists who left was eagerly bought up by the other farmers to increase their acreage. Most of the families are rapidly getting out of debt; the colony is now self-supporting and operating at a profit as a result of its canneries, creameries, agricultural products. There is more of a demand for "Matanuska Maid," the colony trade name, products than the colony can fill.

By 1938 Palmer had electricity, telephone, an excellent road system, post office, garage, a hatchery, beauty shop and barber, a modern hospital and several stores and restaurants. Since then the growth has been steady. The *Valley Settler*, a newspaper, is published weekly.

Although gold had much to do with opening up Alaska and bringing thousands of people north to the Territory, it must now take second place among Alaska's industries. Today fish is king! It is after rounding Alaska Peninsula and heading northward that you come to the shallow arm of Bering Sea, Bristol Bay, one of the richest salmon fishing areas in the world. During the late summer and fall millions of salmon swim in its waters on their way to spawn in its tributary rivers and lakes. With the exception of Nushagak Bay on its northern shore, Bristol Bay was up to 1940 inadequately mapped and sounded. It is believed to be nowhere more than three hundred feet deep.

During the fishing season a fleet of ocean-going vessels, most of which have seen better days, anchors in Bristol Bay and commences operations. Because of the scarcity of local labor, seasonal workers are imported, usually from Puget Sound. A good many of these live on the boats while in Bristol Bay. Labor is also imported for work in the canneries on shore; several floating canneries operate from scows.

Alaskan waters have five species of salmon. The largest is the king, known also as the chinook on the Columbia River, which averages about twenty-two pounds in weight. The Alaska red, known as the sockeye or blueback in other waters, weighs around seven pounds, and prefers rivers that have their headwaters in lakes, or that have lakes along their course. Its flesh is deep red, from which it gets its name. The coho, silver, or medium red salmon, is of a silvery color and usually weighs about eight pounds. The pink salmon is the smallest and most numerous of the species, blue and silver with round black spots on the upper part, and weighs about two pounds. The chum, or keta, is silvery on the sides and sometimes sprinkled with small black specks. It averages about nine pounds and is the cheapest of all salmon, because its meat is of a pale color and sometimes has less oil than other varieties. Paler colored salmons are less fashionable with the public and so cheaper, but experts have pronounced them just as delicious and nourishing as the red-fleshed variety.

Salmon are hatched in fresh water where they remain two years and then descend to the sea. When they migrate outbound they are only a few inches long; but they grow rapidly in salt water and two or three years later, fully grown, they return, "each to the stream where it was born," to spawn and die. It is on this homeward migration that the fish are taken for commercial pur-

Kegs of fish from Bristol Bay being loaded aboard a steamer which will take them to the States

poses. During the few days of the season $12,000,000 worth of salmon is caught in Bristol Bay alone, at normal peace-time prices.

That nearly or quite every fish seeks unerringly the river and the branch stream of its birth and early development, seems so romantic that many have doubted it on that score; besides, it looked incredible that memory, sense of direction, and "instinct" would suffice; for the fish have been abroad in the largest of the world's oceans, the Pacific, to distances of thousands of miles, and this has not been merely a trip but the major part of a lifetime — more than half by years and several score times by weight and size.

Many theories were developed to aid in the explanation of the unerring return, one of them that the salmon has a delicate temperature sense and is guided thereby, more or less automatically, somewhat as plants turn toward or away from the sun. It was said, for instance, that when a migration comes to the forks of a river the division of those that go up one stream against those following the other depends on comparative warmth, the larger number ascending the chillier stream. But further studies make it seem increasingly probable that this type of mechanistic theory, though not without force, is only a small part of the explanation. In the present state of knowledge it does seem as if the salmon traveled by a homing instinct — instinct being our name for a behavior we do not understand.

At Naknek, a fishing village on the northeastern shore of Bristol Bay, they have a fleet of about five motor-driven barges instead of the usual barge and tugboat combination used in Alaska for getting supplies ashore from ocean-going vessels. These have been used successfully in all kinds of weather and, unlike ordinary barges, can operate in what the Alaskans call "big" weather, which means a storm with a high sea.

Between Bristol Bay and Cook Inlet is Iliamna Lake, largest in Alaska. Only a few feet above sea level, it was named Shelekof by the Russians as early as 1802, but is now universally known as Iliamna, the native name of a mythical great blackfish, which lives in the lake, and bites holes in the kayaks of bad natives.

Next to Bristol Bay Ketchikan is probably the most important fishing center in Alaska. It is the second largest town and stands on Revillagigedo Island, one of the incredible number that make up the Alexander Archipelago, as those islands that border the Panhandle are called. Vancouver in 1793 named

148

Ketchikan, first port of entry into Alaska, 750 miles north of Seattle

this strange sounding island after the Viceroy of Mexico, Revilla Gigedo and most people find it difficult to pronounce all in one breath.

A leading port, Ketchikan's harbor is crowded with hundreds of colorful fishing boats that make it their home port. It is one of the most important halibut and salmon fishing centers in Alaska and its nine canneries pack from 300,000 to 500,000 forty-eight-can cases of salmon each year. Most of the canning is now done by automatic machinery, a far cry from the early canning days when tins were hand-made and the fish was cleaned, cut into pieces and packed by hand. In addition to canned salmon, millions of pounds of fish are frozen in Ketchikan's modern cold storage plant, both for food and bait.

Ketchikan, with a population of almost 5,000 in 1940, has an annual average temperature of 45°. As to heat, the summers are like those along the coast of Maine. Very little snow falls in winter but it rains and rains, winter and summer. Most of Ketchikan's houses, built mainly of spruce and cedar, have gardens both front and back bursting with color. Delphiniums are eight or nine feet high and the pansies grow as big as saucers.

Ketchikan is usually the first Alaskan town visited by tourists who come north by boat. Through islands of green forest, gliding along mirror-still water comes the ship until suddenly it rounds another bend and there is Ketchikan. Built against Deer Mountain and a neighboring hill the town is divided by a waterfall. A typical American Main Street crowded with jostling crowds and parked automobiles runs down to the water's edge. It usually has a sign which says "Welcome Visitors" hung across its middle. The streets have wooden sidewalks and at the Blue Fox Bar juke boxes play the same tunes they were playing when you left home. There are no highways leading out of Ketchikan but there are plenty of automobiles which drive in and around the town. Like so many Alaskan towns built on the water's edge in Alaska, Ketchikan is isolated from all land communication.

ALASKA'S FARTHEST NORTH

A glance at a polar projection map of the northern hemisphere, or at the top of a globe, shows the countries of the north grouped around a smallish sea, named the Arctic Ocean; it is descriptively called the Polar Mediterranean, for it lies between its surrounding countries somewhat as the Old World Mediterranean lies between Europe and Africa.

Our most northerly cape on the Polar Mediterranean is Point Barrow, the northernmost spot in Alaska. As the planes fly it is five hundred miles northeasterly from Nome and five hundred northwesterly from Fairbanks. Nuvuk, meaning the "point," is the native name of the all-Eskimo village here. Captain Beechey, in 1826, named the point after Sir John Barrow, a great patron of exploration, who was responsible for Parliament's offering the twenty-thousand-pound reward to the first navigator sailing the Northwest Passage. Although it appears as Point Barrow on the map, it is still Nuvuk to the natives, about eighty-two of whom have their village on the end of the point.

Point Barrow is about twelve miles northward of Barrow, a post office

Salmon Canneries just north of Ketchikan

and settlement. Here in 1940 there were one hundred and eleven families, four of whom were white. It is an important trading post. A well-stocked store is run by Charlie Brower, now in his eighties, who has resided there since 1884 and probably knows more about the Arctic coast of Alaska than anyone living. He is not only the storekeeper, he is the friend of everyone who has ever visited Barrow and one of the most famous Alaskans. Many explorers have been his guest and their narratives contain affectionate stories about him.

While a few trading vessels call at Barrow during the season of navigation, landing is a difficult and often hazardous operation. Lighters, which are large open boats, or barges, are kept at hand and in typical Alaskan fashion, supplies are taken ashore.

Formerly all travel around Point Barrow in winter, and all winter trips to Barrow, were by dog sled. During the early part of Alaskan reindeer domestication a few deliveries of mail to this northernmost American post office were by reindeer sledge—this was while the reindeer was still looked upon in considerable part as a draft animal and before Alaskans had arrived at the conclusions that, in this country, it is chiefly valuable for its meat and skins.

But now, as everywhere in Alaska, the chief means of travel is the airplane. Barrow has seen the arrival and departure of many important exploratory flights. In 1925 Wilkins made from there and Fairbanks the first airplane flight over the Polar Sea from an American base. In 1926 the dirigible *Norge*, piloted by its builder Umberto Nobile, with the Norwegian commander Amundsen and the American second-in-command Ellsworth, reached Barrow on its flight from Spitsbergen by way of the North Pole to Teller, Alaska.

In 1927 Wilkins and the Alaska aviation pioneer Eielson made from Barrow an epoch-making flight in that it was the first on which a plane with either skiis or wheels landed on and took off from the pack ice far from shore; for they made three safe landings, two of them 500 miles northwest from Barrow and the third 100 miles north from Barrow. The last descent was followed by a ten-day drift eastward parallel to the coast of Alaska and then by a hundred-mile walk ashore. This flight is considered by many to be the most important of all Arctic airplane flights in that it destroyed a belief which had previously been a serious handicap to the development of northern aviation, that the ice of the Polar Sea was unsuited to emergency landings and takeoffs.

In 1928 Wilkins and Eielson made from Barrow the first airplane crossing of the Polar Mediterranean, as distinguished from flights part way into it and then back again to where you started from. On their flight from Barrow to Spitsbergen they went about 200 miles out of their way to avoid flying over the North Pole. For this they had two chief reasons, that they did not want their crossing to be mistaken for one more North Pole flight, and they wanted to traverse on the way as much unexplored ocean as possible. Had they flown by way of the Pole they would have repeated, between Barrow and the Pole, the flight of the *Norge* two years before. At the pole itself they would have been the fourth group of visitors—Peary by sledge in 1909, Byrd by airplane in 1926, and Amundsen-Ellsworth-Nobile by dirigible also in 1926.

The Wilkins-Eielson crossing of the Polar Sea remained the only one for nine years, until in 1937 came the two flights from Moscow to the United States by way of the North Pole.

In 1937 Barrow was one of several bases for search operations in quest of the lost Soviet flyer, Levanevsky. Sir Hubert Wilkins, in charge of the American side of the operations, flew in this search a total of 45,440 miles, about three quarters of which was north of the Arctic Circle and more than 20,000 miles of it over the Polar Sea. Ten thousand miles of these flights were in winter, between November and March, some of them wholly by night, which meant a two-thousand-mile flight during which no glint of daylight was ever seen by the flyers who depended on the stars for guidance and on the moon for light. The search did not clear up the mystery of Levanevsky's fate, but it advanced the cause of Arctic flying notably.

The U.S. Government school at Barrow is our own most northerly, and is farther north than any school in Canada or Greenland, though not so far north as some schools in the Soviet Union. It has a Presbyterian mission. A government hospital was built in 1939.

Barrow is in truly Arctic country. It is 330 miles north of the Arctic Circle and far from any warm current such as the Gulf Stream waters that flow at the same latitude past the north coast of Norway. In great masses pressed forward by a resistless current, about the heaviest ice pack known from any part of the world grinds right by its front door. The village stands on permanently frozen sub-soil in which the people dig storage chambers that will keep meat fresh for years. In summer the thaw goes down only from six to eighteen inches but there is abundant grass on this top soil.

At Barrow you reach permanent frost at the end of summer if you dig two feet down, but the meadows of grass formerly supported vast herds of caribou and they now support steadily growing herds of their domestic cousins the reindeer. Nor is the farthest tip of the northernmost sandspit the end of Alaska's resources. Yankee whalers learned a century ago that fortunes could be built in Massachusetts from whale oil and whale bone that came from the sea to the north of Alaska. Stefansson proved on his journeys between 1914 and 1918 that the riches of the sea do not stop where vessels cease being able to pursue the whale northward, for his parties lived by hunting as they traveled afoot over the pack ice many hundreds of miles north from Alaska. Papanin and his colleagues demonstrated in 1937 that the waters are rich with plant and animal life at the

153

geographic pole, more than a thousand miles north from Barrow. Fifty years ago Peary described butterflies and bumblebees on the north coast of Greenland, across the full diameter of the northern sea from Barrow. Wilkins and the Soviet flyers have been proving to us again and again that the Arctic Mediterranean, between the Old World and the New, is in climate and conditions particularly suited for air transport.

All of this means that the north coast of Alaska is not a limit to northward progress, nor the shore of an ocean that is desolate. There is little doubt that, when peace returns, a network of aerial commerce will bind Alaska with northern Europe, Arctic Canada with northern Siberia.

To the south of Alaska are the resources of the Pacific Ocean, of British Columbia and the Pacific States. To the west of Alaska are Bristol Bay, with its greatest of salmon fisheries, and Bering Sea, wealthy with cod, haddock and halibut, walrus and seal. On that side, too, Alaska is near Japan and near the rapidly developing Soviet Union. On her north she faces Europe and northwestern Asia across the smallest of the oceans, the Arctic Ocean, highway of the future for aerial commerce. To the east her frontier is against northwestern Canada, whose Mackenzie Valley contains more known reserves of petroleum than all the rest of the world combined, a life blood that can pour into Alaska's commercial veins through short arteries of steel pipe.

As we have said, Alaska has within her borders the climate of Denmark in her south, the climate of Finland in her north, an area greater than that of Finland and all the Scandinavian countries, and resources greater than those of Finland and the Scandinavias. Alaska has the location, the size and the resources to make her in population and wealth greater than the combined Scandinavias!

There are not many now who call Alaska "Seward's Folly" except to deride those who thought the Purchase a folly. If you speak of it as "Seward's Ice Box," you do so with a modern appreciation of the value, the comfort and utility of ice. To those that know Alaska, and they grow more numerous each year, it is the "Land of Tomorrow."

Two belles in their fancy dress "parky's"

St. Mary's Seminary-Junior College

SIBERIA

ARCTIC

ARC

Wrangel Is.

Pt. Hope

Kotzebue S.

Diomede Is.

Cape Pri
Port Clare
Nome

BERING

BERING SEA

St Lawrence Is.

Norton Sound

Date

A DEORATI
ALAS
showing its principal ports, cities,
and islands. Also showing its relation to
the Arctic Circle, Siberia and Aleutians.

Near
Is.

Kiska
Is.

A

Atka Is.

EUTIAN ISLANDS

P   CIFIC

Unalaska
Is.

Dutch Harbor

Unimak Is.

Bristol
Under about
center of th
cartouche are the
Pribilof Is.